BEATING ANGER

The eight-point plan for coping with rage

Mike Fisher

RIDER

LONDON · SYDNEY · AUCKLAND · JOHANNESBURG

7 9 10 8

Fi ... publis ... ... of Ebury ... ss,
Ra ... on House, ... ndon SW1 ... SA

Addresses ... or companies ... ... ouse Group ... n be found at
www. ... .com

... om House Group ... ...

Printed and b ... ... lin by ... rman Ltd, Rea ... g, Berkshire

A CIP ca ... ... cord for this boo ... ... h Library

ISBN 9781844135646

The Random House Group Limited supports The Forest Stewardship
Council (FSC), the leading international forest certification organisation.
All our titles that are printed on Greenpeace approved FSC certified paper
carry the FSC logo. Our paper procurement policy can be found at:
www.rbooks.co.uk/environment

Illustration on page 47 extracted from *Brain Story* by Susan Greenfield
reproduced with the permission of BBC Worldwide Limited.
Illustration Copyright © BBC Worldwide Limited 2000

Lines from *Rumi – Hidden Music* translated by Maryam Mafi & Azima Melita
Kolin © 2001 reprinted by kind permission of HarperCollins Publishers Ltd.
Every effort has been made to contact all copyright holders, but if any have
been inadvertently overlooked, then the author and publisher will make the
necessary arrangements at the first opportunity.

Contents

Introduction

Sloth, apathy and despair are the enemy, anger is not. Anger is our friend. Not a nice friend, not a gentle friend but a very loyal friend. It will always tell you when you have been betrayed. It will always tell when we have betrayed ourselves. It will always tell us that it is time to act in our own best interests. Anger is not the action itself, it is action's invitation.

—*Elspeth Weymann*

If you have chosen this book, you either have personal experience of anger issues or you know someone who does, and you love and care for them enough to try to understand their behaviour. Anger may be the most complex emotional state a person can enter. If you do not understand the various aspects of anger and find yourself lost in the perpetual cycle of angry feelings, you may eventually drown in your own rage, hate and despair.

This book has been written to help people find a way to deal with the anger in their lives. We will be exploring the many styles of anger and discovering which one applies to you, as well as learning how to recognise an angry person when we see one. Whether you think you have a problem with anger or not, you will find information in these pages that will help you to understand and manage both your own and other people's anger. You may even find yourself becoming a role model for the healthy expression of anger.

So what does an angry person look like? In truth, an angry person can look just like you, me or anyone else you know. Anger isn't just the prerogative of those who make the newspapers; all of us experience it to one degree or other. The issue for those of us who have a problem with anger is not that we *feel* anger; it is the way that we *express* our anger that leads to hurtful or harmful episodes – for all concerned. We need to learn how to deal with anger and understand its rightful purpose in our lives.

This book is both educational and experiential. As well as infor-mation, it includes exercises designed to question your beliefs and challenge your logic, exposing mistaken notions and perhaps even distorted thinking patterns. Through completing these exercises you will begin to gain a clearer understanding of yourself and discover tools that will equip you to deal more positively with any potential conflict situation in the future. Your task is to study this book and make your anger a personal project. If you do this, the book will become a powerful vehicle for transforming your life.

My story

I know the suffering that anger can inflict. Indeed, it was my own struggle with anger that led me to work in the field of anger management. My anger was the final stumbling block to my becoming psychologically healthy and emotionally stable.

In my early teens, although I often felt angry, I quickly stifled strong angry feelings because I felt scared of them. I thought that if I expressed them my friends would not like me. I started to believe that, apart from the Incredible Hulk, I was probably the most angry person in existence, since no one seemed to speak about or openly express their feelings of anger. Initially, my anger wasn't explosive; it was implosive. By this I mean that I turned my anger in on myself, which manifested directly as depression and indirectly as self-harming behaviour, such as smoking too much dope, with all its physical and psychological consequences.

One of my outlets for my frustration and rage was through art. I feverishly expressed myself in drawing. Later, I started having relationships with girls and began to take my anger out on them, not through physical aggression but through cruel and pathological game-playing. I was terrified of allowing people to come too close to me. I became ashamed of who I was and ashamed of my behaviour, but I could not recognise that I needed to change or, indeed, that change was even possible.

The way I expressed anger during these implosive years was passive aggressive (we will explore this further on page 24). I came across as being very superior, judgmental and critical of others. I would never suggest that I was angry with them. Instead, I would make sarcastic, cynical and patronising comments to wind them up deliberately. And if I didn't do this, I would spread rumours about them, talk behind their backs and generally do whatever I could to hurt them.

Even when I started training as a counsellor, in my early thirties, I avoided overtly expressing my anger. Confrontations where out of the question. (Occasionally, I still find myself behaving in that way today, despite now being much more comfortable with my own and other people's anger.) Then when I qualified, I managed to work only with those therapists who were not challenging and confrontational – 'nice' therapists – because my fear of dealing with my anger was so great. I remember thinking once that the world would be a much better place if people simply did not have angry feelings. I for one would certainly be more comfortable and much happier! When I look back now I have to laugh at myself. How could I possibly have thought it would be so much easier if angry feelings were eradicated? I have certainly come a long way since then.

When I was in my late thirties I reached a turning point. Someone I cared for, and believed cared for me, betrayed me – or so I believed. Now I realise that in fact I set myself up for betrayal. I went completely ballistic. I was on the rampage for months – like a bear with a sore head and a bruised ego. Years's worth of imploded anger rose to the surface. I felt invincible; nothing could touch me or get at me. I no longer cared what other people thought of me; in fact, I believed it didn't matter what other people thought of me. My anger came out whenever and wherever. I was completely out of control but, boy oh boy, was I having fun with this new-found power inside me!

Unfortunately, I never considered the effect that my anger was having on other people. I didn't see that having experienced my anger they became afraid of me, lost their respect for me and no longer took me seriously. Only after the dust had settled and I peered out from behind my protective armour plating did I begin to see the devastation I had left behind. Suddenly I realised that I had crossed a line.

At this point, I spoke to one of my mentors. I have never forgotten what he said to me: 'Sometimes we have to experience the polarity of things in order to define where we need to live.' I understood this to mean that having lived as an imploder for many years and then having become an exploder, I finally had the means to gain an inkling of what I needed to do in order to express my anger appropriately.

This book is about that journey – a journey that we all have to take. It's about understanding the theory, the nuts and bolts, and the application of the theory, so that we can manage our anger well.

How this book works

This book is written in two parts. The first part is about understanding your anger, and the second part looks at managing your anger.

People often think there's nothing much to understand about anger, but in reality anger is staggeringly complex. In Part One you will begin to discover the basic elements of anger, what activates it and the role that it plays in our lives. This section describes our defence mechanisms, offering an insight into how sophisticated they may become when we are trying to avoid feeling pain. It includes an explanation of the basic functions of the brain in relation to the fight, flight and freeze mechanism, which will help you to understand why managing and expressing anger appropriately is challenging. We will be discussing how our primary needs come into play, and how you can take responsibility for getting those needs met. The concept of shadow projections and how they act as one of the major triggers for anger will also be explained. Then, once you have some understanding of how and why we get angry, we will also look at the five different styles of anger, the role power plays in our relationships, the difference between imploders and exploders, and the difference between clean and unclean ways of expressing our anger.

In a way, Part One of the book is the detective work. By doing the exercises it contains, you will begin to become aware of your inner thoughts, emotions, ideas, beliefs, behaviours and actions. Each chapter will invoke lots of feelings in you – feelings that will excite you and that may also reawaken feelings of shame, sadness, fear and, of course, anger as you slowly come to terms with the effects of your past experiences. You will be travelling deep into yourself and learning what is really going on with you. At times this may be frightening. Remember that what you are really doing is venturing away from old harmful modes of operating.

Part Two of the book is about learning skills to manage and control your anger. An in-depth section on emotional trauma will help you to clarify your experiences and the ways in which you can heal historical trauma. From this you will learn to distinguish whether the degree of your anger is appropriate or not. We will discuss the eight golden rules of anger management in detail. These rules will become the principles that you need to remember once you have completed this book. Each rule provides context and tools for managing your anger, and each can stand alone or be used together with any or all of the others at any given moment.

Part Two marks the starting point for pulling yourself back together again. You will begin to make connections and have feelings and insights that you have never experienced before. It will stimulate conversations with loved ones, perhaps even inspiring you to talk to your parents (if they are still alive), as the information they can offer to supplement your own memories will help you to unravel your experiences and make sense of your feelings. Getting together with your siblings and discussing some of the concepts you have read here may offer further clarification of what actually makes you tick. If you absorb the material in these pages and apply it to your life by the end of the book you will have all the tools you need to control your anger.

At this point I feel it's important to say that this book will *not* make you stop feeling angry – although it will probably make you feel angry a great deal less often. Anger is a natural and healthy emotion, if we skillfully manage how we use it. It is an emotion that can completely cloud our judgement, but it doesn't have to be this way. Through understanding the nature of anger you can turn it into your ally rather than your enemy.

Mike Fisher
December 2004

Useful Tools

The following are suggestions for tools that will help to support you as you work through this book.

Build a support network – anger buddies

Developing and building into your daily life a support network of anger buddies is invaluable when you are working on managing your anger. Anger is probably the most volatile of all our feelings and can therefore be the most difficult to understand and harness, so the encouragement and support of others can be of enormous help.

Throughout the book I will be referring to using your support network. We will be looking at the importance of support and how it fits into your overall anger management strategy in more detail in Chapter Seven (see pages 236–9). Here I want to suggest some ways of enroling anger buddies into your programme – now is a good time to start thinking about who might be able to offer you support. Once you have your support network in place, you will find it much easier to work through the book and follow the programme. These people will become your life-line to health and emotional wellbeing.

I understand that as a result of your problem with managing anger many of you will have isolated yourselves from others. Of course, this makes finding and receiving support that much more difficult. Don't become disillusioned; you can begin with just one individual. They will themselves gain much from this process, so you will both grow from the experience. After all, anger is a fascinating subject, and one that concerns us all.

So what does support look like in the case of anger management? In essence, you will need people who you trust and who can be relied upon, people who are responsible and accountable. They will be people who will not tell you what you want to hear but what you need to hear, and if you have been irresponsible in your anger, they will encourage you to rectify the situation.

Take some time to think about whom you could ask to be your anger buddy and then sit down and write some notes about how you could use them as support. Ultimately, it's up to you to identify possible buddies from those around you and ask them for support, but the following are suggestions for people you could ask:

* A good friend
* A close relative
* A family member
* Your doctor
* A therapist
* Members of a therapy group
* A worker on a helpline, such as Samaritans or Sane Line
* Your priest, rabbi or other religious leader

Ideally, you need to recruit at least eight people to your support network, as they may not be available all the time. It may take a while to build your network, but for now at least begin the process of engaging with the possibility and making enquiries.

Keep a journal

Another way of supporting yourself through the anger management process is to keep a notebook with you at all times, especially while reading this book. Many of the exercises require a written response, and you may want to jot down new thoughts and feelings that come to you. This notebook will serve as your journal – a sort of inner camera for your feelings. Capture your thoughts and, if you like, share them with an anger buddy.

Journal keeping needs to become a habit. I use my own journal to make a note of feelings, thoughts and reflections that are important in my life. I also use it as a cathartic tool to purge myself of negative thoughts, feelings and fantasies. My journals have become a testament of my journey as well as a way of helping me to stay focused on emotional issues in my life.

Chapter Seven contains more information on keeping an anger management journal, suggesting ways of giving structure and focus to your journalling and providing a list of questions you can ask yourself in order to get started.

Learn to listen

Another tool to consider is your ability to listen. Do you listen to others when they speak or do you tend to interrupt them? Do you speak over them? Do you only pretend to take in what they are saying?

Begin now to become a better listener. Really make a point of listening to others. Becoming a better listener will help you to become a better and more effective learner. By listening more you will hear things you have not heard before. You will make space for others around you to be heard, including your children, your spouse, your employees and so on. Try asking them what they think about things or how they feel.

One of the most effective tools for communication is very simple: let one person speak at a time! I often find that when I am angry, the other person cannot get a word in edgeways. Learning to listen and allowing only one person to speak without interruption creates space for open, healthy dialogue.

A word of advice

Please be aware that reading this book may stir up a lot of uncomfortable feelings for you. These may have historical content or they may relate to a present-day situation. I urge you to be patient and allow this material to settle before deciding to act upon it. Often those I work with believe that once something comes to the surface they have to deal with it immediately. It is much more productive to do the following: open your journal and make a few notes or, if past memories have come to the surface, write them down, together with any added insights, in lots of detail. Then allow your anger buddy to read through what you have written. Talk through your feelings with them until you know you have a deeper clarity on the issues with which you are faced. This in itself may be enough to bring an issue to resolution, but should you decide that you need to take up an issue with someone, follow the procedures described on pages 213–18. Make sure that you use the time with the person to heal things between you, not to make things worse. This process is not about going on a witch hunt; it's about making friends with your demons.

Sometimes when we re-visit our previous hurts, the feelings that arise can be overwhelming. Try to be gentle with yourself. Give yourself permission to feel these things without pushing or rushing yourself to get over them. Allow yourself the time and space, knowing that in the end this is all about bringing something to a close so that it no longer haunts you. Reach out to your support network as much as possible and allow yourself to receive their support. Should you feel the need for professional support, find yourself a good counsellor or therapist to work with, ideally someone with lots of experience and a good grounding in anger management. You will find a list of resources on page 261.

PART ONE
Understanding Anger

Until one is committed, there is hesitancy, the chance to draw back, always ineffectiveness. Concerning all acts of initiative (and creation), there is one elementary truth the ignorance of which kills countless ideas and splendid plans; that the moment one definitely commits oneself, then providence moves too. All sorts of things occur to help one that would never otherwise have occurred. A whole stream of events issues from the decision, raising in one's favour all manner of unforeseen incidents and meetings and material assistance, which no man could have dreamed would come his way. Whatever you can do or dream you can, begin it. Boldness has genius, power and magic in it. Begin it now.

— *Johan Wolfgang von Goethe,*
The Power of Commitment

CHAPTER 1

Defining Anger

It is astonishing to observe how anger is commonly portrayed in the media. Headlines often attempt to grab our attention by naming and shaming some unfortunate angry individual as dysfunctional, outrageous, shameful, crazed and out of control. We as a society tend to take the same attitudes. Hence, anger is often considered to be something bad, wrong or inappropriate rather than a legitimate response to certain situations. As a society, the way we generally deal with anger is to deny its existence, to disassociate from our anger and then blame someone else when it erupts in our face. In our culture, we are too afraid to face the heat of anger directly, both in ourselves and in others. Let's take a closer look at some of the issues surrounding anger in society today.

Is our society getting angrier?

When I speak to the media, I am often asked if our society is becoming angrier. I do not believe that this is the case. If it feels that way, it is because anger is documented more now than ever before in history. In 2003 there was even a mainstream Hollywood film called *Anger Management*, starring Jack Nicholson and Adam Sandler. Anger is everywhere on television, in our newspapers and on the radio. And yet anger has been around for thousands of years and pondered by many philosophers. It is a fundamental aspect of the human condition.

The way that anger is allowed to be expressed, however, shifts and changes throughout the ages. For many years in Britain, explicitly expressed anger has been socially frowned upon (while passive aggression has gone unchecked). Now it seems that this is changing. We have gone from being a nation of imploders, turning our anger inwards, to being a nation of exploders, turning our anger outwards.

Unexpressed anger takes its toll. After years of keeping their anger inside, chronic imploders frequently end up needing medication, either to go on suppressing their anger or to deal with the impact suppression has had on their health. Exploders, too, can suffer from health problems, but, by and large, anger expressed is much healthier than anger left on the slow burner. The problem is its consequences for those around us. An exploder drops his bombshell and then ten minutes later is OK – but what about the person on the receiving end? It can take hours, days, weeks, months or even years for them to recover from the blast.

Are men angrier than women?

This question evokes a certain amount of controversy. Some theorists believe that men and women are equally angry – goodness knows we all have reason enough to be. Judging by the conversations I have had with thousands of participants in anger management courses over the last five years, I have come to the conclusion that women are generally angrier than men. My view is that if you are a woman living under the influence of patriarchy, you have much more reason to be angry. That is not to say that men have not been affected negatively by patriarchal values – of course they have. The difference is that men typically have many more avenues for venting their anger, including war, cut-throat business, combat, extreme sports, play-fighting, hunting, aggression and even domestic violence (which is often minimised and normalised in our culture). For men the venting of anger is generally encouraged by society and reinforced by the media.

For many generations of women, however, acceptability has been contingent on their repressing their anger. Only in the last 150 years or so have women fought both politically and socially for equality and a voice. Perhaps it's not so much that women are angrier than men, but that they are now – finally – allowing themselves to express their anger more openly as they begin to assert themselves in the world. Women's anger tends to be more visible because we are not used to seeing women express their anger forthrightly. Indeed, I often come across men on my programmes who are surprised to find women attending an anger management programme, believing that women don't get angry! Usually around 55 per cent of the participants on my courses are men, while around 45 per cent are women.

Are our children angrier than we were?

My own personal conclusion is that children today are more angry than we were. Indeed, I receive thousands of phone calls from desperate parents seeking help for their children. The reason why young people are so angry is partly to do with their high consumption of fast foods and partly to do with a lack of healthy adult role models for them to look up to. Children often get mixed messages from their parents – especially the ones that say, 'Do as I say, not as I do'. This is very confusing for a child, and out of this confusion comes hurt, fear and then anger. Children can also suffer profound pain because parents and teachers lack the emotional literacy to understand why children may start behaving in ways that are destructive.

When assessing a child for help with anger management, I always inform the parents that we will need to work on their relationship to their own anger and talk about their parenting skills. Parents often believe – wrongly – that if their children are angry they have themselves failed somehow. Because they do not want to admit this to anyone else – and sometimes because they are in denial about their own anger issues and project them onto their children – they cannot take advantage of the help that is offered. Any issue involving a child can have dramatic effects on the family as a whole. A lot of attention will usually be focused on the 'problem' child, which only adds to the child's sense of shame, guilt and despair.

When working with children, it is crucial to keep in mind that all behaviour is learnt. Anger management needs to be taught in every school across the land, to children, teachers and parents, as part of the national curriculum. Many teachers know this to be true, but very few schools – and then usually only as a last resort, born out of pure desperation – offer training in these skills.

The ten basic ingredients for managing dispute in our lives

Considering the lack of education and tolerance of anger in our society, it's no wonder there is such a problem with the management of this powerful feeling. Anger is scary, but the denial of it only makes it stronger. With this in mind, I have created a list of ten basic ingredients required for managing dispute in our lives. These are considerations that you need to understand in order to manage conflict in a more productive way.

Have you noticed that when you get into an angry conflict with someone close to you, at some point during the argument you often discover that actually both of you want the same thing? When you finally say to the other person, 'So what is it that you want from me?', they reply, 'I want you to value and respect me!', and you find yourself saying in return, 'That's exactly what I want from you!' I have found in almost every personal conflict that people basically want the same things; they just have dysfunctional ways of going about getting them. In essence, we all have certain primary needs – such as the need to be loved and the need to be respected – and when these needs are not being met our anger is triggered.

The next time you find yourself in conflict consider the following:

1 We all see and hear the things we want to see and hear.

2 What we assume or take for granted is often incorrect.

3 Happiness is a choice.

4 Conflict is a necessary part of maturing emotionally.

5 It's your choice.

6 You can change.

7 Learning positive strategies to manage anger increases our ability to be intimate.

8 We are all multi-faceted.

9 We all need to feel understood.

10 We all need to communicate.

Let's go through those points in a little more detail.

1 We all see and hear the things we want to see and hear

Rather than seeing and hearing things the way they are, we dissemble, distort and manipulate reality so that it fits in with what we've come to expect. We do this in order to create safety for ourselves in the world, because what we're used to, good or bad, is comfortable for us.

Each of us has a very specific experience of reality, made up of our past, our present and our foreseeable future. Your model of reality or subjective experience is certainly not the same as anyone else's. It is important to remember this and to acknowledge and validate each person's individual reality. A common problem for people who have difficulty managing their anger is that they cannot quite accept that people have different realities. Recognising this can often be the first step in dissolving anger.

Have you ever wondered why on certain days you can roll with what life throws at you, while on other days you feel as if everything is falling apart? Moment by moment, our capacity to deal with events depends on our emotional state of being. We are all constantly shifting through different states of feeling, whether we are aware of them or not. How, then, can you realistically expect others to be different? Sure, we all have similar needs, wants and desires, but the way we react to them and the way we see our reality depends on the way we are feeling in the moment.

This simple truth is the key to much pain and conflict in our lives. We want people to fit into our own model of subjective reality even though it is not theirs, and we waste a great deal of time and energy trying to convince them that they should be more like us. Meanwhile, they're all trying to do the same! Needless to say, things just don't work this way. The task in managing conflict is to respect other people's world view and to find a way of agreeing to disagree.

2 What we assume or take for granted is often incorrect

In most disputes there are assumptions flying around – and with assumptions come expectations, and with expectations come resentments just waiting to bubble to the surface.

Always do a reality check before making an assumption (remember, when you assume you make an 'ass' of 'u' and 'me').

This also means that when you take someone for granted, you are assuming that their needs are not as important as your own – enough to make anyone angry! Thus it is very important to check out with the other person what they really need and feel in the moment.

Take the view that to other people nothing is obvious and be very clear about your own thoughts, feelings, needs and desires. Don't assume that people can read your mind. I often find in my one-to-one work that certain clients expect their partner (or other people close to them) to be a mind-reader; if the partner fails at this, it becomes another bone of contention in the relationship.

Just because our mother may have known how to anticipate our infant needs, it does not mean that anyone else can or will. We certainly shouldn't expect them to. It's important that you are clear about what you want, and that you learn how to *ask* for it. Making assumptions is essentially immature behaviour and reflects a certain amount of resistance to growing up and taking responsibility for ourselves.

3 Happiness is a choice

This is the title of a wonderful book by Bill Kauthman about his experience of having a child with special needs. In this book he suggests that just because your child has special needs and does not function in the world in the way you want him to, does not mean you have to be unhappy. We can apply this concept to anger management. Just because you are angry with me, it does not mean I have to be angry or unhappy with you. It just means you are angry with me. I do not have to become like you, nor do I have to take responsibility for your anger (although I may empathise or show compassion).

A few years ago, I noticed that when I had seen clients I would often come home in a jolly good mood. When I asked my wife how she was, she would tell me how unhappy she felt because of the challenges of the day, and my mood would change instantly to fit hers. This happened without my even knowing it. Once I had become aware of this, I decided to take note of every time I shifted into another mood gear and try to make a choice to remain happy. And it worked. It was quite hard in the early stages, but eventually I got the hang of it.

Your happiness does not depend on whether those around you are happy or not; it depends on whether *you* are happy or not. You can make a choice to be happy in the moment, moment by moment, and commit to sticking to this choice. When your spouse or your child or your boss is in a grumpy mood, this does not mean that you also have to be in a grumpy mood; it just means that they are. You can remain in the mood you're in, without having to feel that you are not being sensitive to their needs.

4 Conflict is a necessary part of maturing emotionally

No pain, no gain, so the saying goes. Part of being human is to experience anger and express it accordingly, as with any other feeling. In our early years we face conflict as a natural part of our existence, and our parents or primary carers are either equipped to deal with our anger or not. If carers are themselves not comfortable with conflict, they will either try to shut it down in us or punish us – with the result, in either case, that our relationship to disputes, disagreements, arguments and conflict in general becomes dysfunctional. Thus many of us have come to equate anger and conflict with pain.

If this is the case for you, it is critical that you reframe your relationship to conflict. It is only through facing up to conflict that we can become more intimate with others. If I cannot express my angry feelings towards you, and you cannot express yours towards me, then our ability to be close is stunted by our fear of hurting each other or ourselves. Dr Carl Jung, the founding father of transpersonal psychology, suggests that in order to grow we need something to push against. The task is to push in a way that both determines and increases our self-awareness and consciousness. By being able to communicate our angry feelings we can grow and become more emotionally mature.

Everything depends on *how* we communicate our feelings. The most effective way I have found of communicating angry feelings in a safe way is by using what I call 'the clearing process'. We will be discussing this in detail in Chapter Six.

5 It's your choice

You can deal with conflict with a knee-jerk reaction or with a more positive form of learned behaviour. The choice is always yours, even though at times it may not feel like it.

According to behavioural psychologists, all behaviour is learned, even when it feels instinctive and out of control. This means that we can learn to stop ourselves over-reacting and to respond in appropriate and creative ways.

We react rather than respond because anger equals pain, and where there is pain, our defence mechanisms kick in involuntarily to avoid it. Until we make the conscious choice to change, all our behaviour will be dominated by reflex reactions.

When you find yourself reacting unhelpfully to situations, you need to focus your attention on this self-destructive behaviour pattern and do something about it. The best way to do this is by using the detour method (see page 170) or and the eight golden rules of anger management (see page 219).

6 You can change

With choice comes the responsibility of sticking with it. Ask yourself, 'Do I want to make changes in my life or do I just want to pay lip service to the healing process?' In order to change you have to really want to. If you simply want to read a book on anger management for the sake of reading, well, that's fine, but if you have an anger problem and you are serious about dealing with it, my suggestion would be that you really take your time with this book and do all the exercises and tasks thoroughly. Investing time and energy in understanding your behaviour will increase your capacity to develop more choices in your life, so enabling you to change destructive and self-defeating behaviours. The knowledge that you can change will help to bring value and meaning to your life and the lives of those around you and will also increase your self esteem.

7 Learning positive strategies to manage anger increases our ability to be intimate

Managing anger is all about supporting ourselves in learning to reduce the number of times we find ourselves in reaction to events and situations and to increase the number of times we can respond in healthy, respectful ways towards others generally. By being less reactive you will reduce the amount of stress you experience, thus becoming more relaxed and happy – and you will live longer for it.

Learning how to respond effectively will make you more popular. People will love to be around you. Rather than feeling afraid of you because of your inconsistent and threatening behaviour, people will want to be closer to you. Of course, to reach this stage takes guts, perseverance, discipline and a commitment to your own wellbeing and emotional health, but it is possible. Many people before you have done it, and you can do it too.

8 We are all multi-faceted

Each one of us is unique in the way that we respond to situations. Moreover, none of us responds to the same situation in the same way all the time. We need to respect our own and others' complexity. This is often where we become stuck – we assume that people are going to remain constant. Remember that the only thing that is constant is our inconsistency. Our reactions to situations is determined by many factors, including our personal history. I myself have changed a remarkable amount over the past 18 years. For example, I never used to get angry when someone arrived late to a meeting or workshop; in recent years, however, this has started to annoy me. This has to do with my discovery that lateness can sometimes be a passive-aggressive act and is to do with holding oneself accountable and having respect for other people.

9 We all need to feel understood

One of our primary needs is to be understood (we will be talking more about primary needs in Chapter Two). Feeling that they are misunderstood can make some people go ballistic! From a very young age we cry in order to get attention. Consider the petulant teenager: most of his or her gripes are about not being understood or taken seriously.

The problem for us as adults is that if we don't understand ourselves, we can't expect others to understand us. And why don't we understand ourselves? This is a controversial subject, but I believe we are simply never taught to understand ourselves. In my view, the school system is based not on fostering personal growth or developing potential but on creating more worker bees for trade and industry. To grease the wheels of capitalism. If you teach people about personal power, they derive meaning from *who* they are, not from what they do for a living or how much money they have. So promoting self-understanding is not a priority for educationalists or governments. When I work with personal growth groups, teenagers and adults alike, a common response is, 'How come we are not taught these basic life skills in school?'

The task is to understand who you are and what makes you tick. Through understanding yourself, you take back the power that you have given away. This book will help you gain insight into your own potential and show you how bringing your anger under control makes you more powerful, not less.

10 We all need to communicate

Learning how to communicate your feelings and needs is part of taking responsibility for yourself. When you are bound up in past hurts, it is almost impossible to communicate your feelings to others; everything that emerges from your mouth will be designed to wound the other person. Rather than speaking from this place, try to communicate when you are in your 'adult' state. This means at a time when you are able to think clearly, remain objective and avoid flying off the handle or bulldozing the other person despite the strength of your feelings. When we are in an adult state, we avoid taking things personally, and we are sensitive and receptive to those around us. Conversely, when we are in a child-like state, we are volatile and behave as if no one else exists other than us. (For more on this subject see page 80). In other words, if you do not feel able to communicate from your adult self, you need to take time out until you do.

Once you are ready to communicate, the other person needs to know:

* How you feel
* What you think
* What you want and need
* That you are willing to take responsibility for your own behaviour
* That you are you willing to listen to them and see their side of the story

Most of us will readily agree that it is vitally important to be able to communicate effectively, and yet for many of us communication is very difficult. Learning this crucial skill is a key task in emotional literacy. This book will provide you with some tools to begin the process of communicating more clearly.

As you work through this book you will discover many tools and skills that will help you to put flesh on the bones of the ten basic ingredients. Before you move on in this task, take a moment to congratulate yourself. You have already taken the first steps towards managing your anger; gaining control of your life; and finding greater self-esteem, confidence and strength for the journey ahead.

What is anger?

There is much confusion about what anger is. Anger is a feeling – nothing more and nothing less. It is no more inherently 'good' or 'bad' than any other feeling. We are born with anger, in the same way that we are born with fear, joy and sadness. We all know what these feelings are like without having to be told. Of all the feelings, anger is, without a doubt, the most volatile, destructive and uncontainable – and it has certainly had the worst press.

Although anger is one of our most basic and commonly experienced feelings, it is woefully misunderstood. When participants in anger management groups describe times when they've been angry, more often than not what they're really talking about is not in fact anger but aggression, passive aggression, hostility or rage. In the next few sections of the book, we're going to look at definitions of the different forms that anger takes to enable you to understand what anger is – and what it isn't.

Passive aggression – the velvet dagger

In battle, a dagger can be easily disguised or concealed from view, yet it is just as deadly as a sword. Passive aggression is a masked form of anger that is just as harmful and hurtful as anger that is expressed more overtly.

Passive aggression is buried anger. I also refer to it as anger through the back door. When it comes out it is usually expressed in veiled and indirect ways. While passive in its application, however, it is aggressive in its intent. It is associated with the 'flight' part of the 'fight or flight' response and is the repression or denial of anger – but anger will always find a way out. People who express their anger passively are often scared of overt anger, be it their own or someone else's.

I believe that a person who is behaving passive-aggressively is more dangerous than a person who is more openly aggressive. The reason for this is that it is almost impossible to detect the intent of the passive-aggressive person, whose anger can sometimes be so loaded with material from historical events that it is hard to sort out past from present causes. So much energy has gone into keeping the lid on their anger that it is only a matter of time before they explode or their anger comes out in a hostile and calculating manner. The implications this has for the health of the individual are far more severe than those for a person who expresses their anger more openly. Indeed, over a period of time passive aggression can lead to depression. Fritz Perls, the founder of Gestalt psychotherapy, suggests that 'depression is anger turned inwards'.

Passive-aggression includes a range of behaviours and feelings. Not everyone who is passive-aggressive will express or experience all of them, but all will exhibit some of them sometimes. Passive-aggressive behaviours include the following:

• *Guardedness, secrecy, caginess, withholding*
Examples: the silent treatment, under-the-breath put-downs, avoiding eye-contact, talking behind others' backs, spreading rumours or malicious gossip, writing poison-pen letters, heckling, stealing, dishonesty and graffiti. More severe examples are

kidnapping and elaborate revenge cycles.

● *Calculation, manipulation, deviousness, underhandedness, controlling*
Examples: provoking others into being aggressive and then patronising them; using emotional blackmail; using tears to make others feel sorry for you; using mental or physical ailments to manipulate others into doing what you want them to; arriving late for appointments; undermining authority figures; forgetting to do things for others; playing stupid or innocent; making sexual innuendoes; withholding information, money or resources.

● *Self-sacrifice, self-denial, martyrdom*
Examples: being too 'nice', being over-helpful, undermining yourself by selling yourself short, being self-suffering but always refusing help, often feeling let down by others.

● *Obsession, compulsion, neurosis, fanaticism*
Examples: perfectionism; needing things to be clean, tidy and in order; dieting or eating obsessively; habitual checking of things; imposing ideals onto yourself or others; either/or thinking.

● *Shiftiness, evasion, slipperiness, dodginess, craftiness, deviousness*
Examples: not dealing with crises, avoiding conflict and frustration, not arguing back, becoming phobic, avoidance (putting the phone down on callers, letting the doorbell ring, not responding to urgent emails), blaming and manipulating others, failing to take responsibility for any of your own behaviours.

● *Self-blame, self-judgement, self-criticism, self-shame*
Examples: always saying how sorry you are even when it's

inappropriate, putting yourself down, setting yourself up as the scapegoat, undermining your own integrity, behaving in any self-destructive way that turns your anger against yourself in order to avoid the pain of conflict and criticism by others.

• *Ineffectuality, incompetence, feebleness, hopelessness*
Examples: setting yourself and others up for failure, being co-dependent or dependent on unreliable people for help and support, being accident-prone and clumsy, making silly mistakes, under-achieving, some forms of sexual impotence.

• *Dispassion, inauthenticity, phoniness, insincerity, inability to make decisions, fatalism, defeatism*
Examples: insincere smiles and laughter; a limp handshake; giving the cold shoulder treatment; sitting on the fence while others sort things out; self-medicating with alcohol, drugs, food, nicotine, sex, work, gambling, etc.

EXERCISE
HOW PASSIVE-AGGRESSIVE ARE YOU?

This exercise will uncover your own passive-aggressive behaviour. I suggest that you work through it with someone from your support network. Also keep your journal handy so that you can make notes as you begin to uncover examples of ways in which you behave passive-aggressively. At the end of the process, note how you feel and write this down. Some of you may be very surprised at how passive-aggressive you can be; rather than beating yourself up, however, use this as an opportunity to befriend your own passive aggression. The first step towards being liberated from your behaviour is simply to become more aware of how it plays out in your life.

•

Look back at the bulleted headings above. Now think about your own life. For each heading write down any instances you can think of when you used these particular passive-aggressive behaviours.

•

Once you have completed your list, show it to your anger buddy so that they can give you support and feedback.

•

Show the list to your family and friends to see whether they agree or disagree with you. They may have notice a few behaviours that you have left out which need to be included. (See Chapter Seven for guidance on fielding feedback.)

— ⚡ —

Unhealthy aggression – the desire for power and control

It's important to note that not all aggression is destructive or harmful. Indeed, some aggression is needed to be successful in certain relationships, business and sport. We use healthy aggression to protect ourselves from being physically and psychically attacked. Where the intent is to help or create safety, then aggression should not be considered hostile or destructive. Aggression becomes unhealthy when it is unrestrained and when it is used to intimidate or control.

People who are aggressive may experience mania, hyperactivity, over-excitedness, frenzy and agitation. They may be selfish and lack empathy for others. They may also be vengeful, unforgiving, vindictive, bitter, merciless, cold-hearted or rigid. Aggressive behaviours include the following:

• *Threatening, menacing, intimidating*
Examples: making threatening statements to others about how
you will harm them or their property, raising your voice, finger-
tapping, eye-balling, finger-pointing, fist-shaking, door-slamming,
wearing clothes that reflect an aggressive attitude or outlook,
driving aggressively.

• *Hurtfulness, cruelty, cutting words, wounding, insensitivity,
spite*
Examples: physical violence, abusive language, sarcasm,
dangerous practical jokes, betraying trust, being unempathetic,
shaming someone privately or publicly, patronising others, not
acknowledging the pain you inflict, manipulating, blaming, not
listening.

• *Destructiveness, harshness, viciousness, caustic words*
Examples: damaging public or private property, damaging or
destroying objects, intentionally wasting resources, intentionally
polluting the environment, intentionally destroying a relationship
between two other people, using drugs or alcohol despite knowing
how destructive they are.

• *Bullying, harrasment, hounding, harrying*
Examples: abusing your position of power or authority,
persecuting, pushing or shoving, using money to oppress others,
shouting louder than the other person, playing on people's
weaknesses, deliberately exposing people in order to shame them
publicly, naming and shaming.

• *Blaming, reprimanding, criticism, scolding, rebuking*
Examples: accusing others of doing what in fact you have done,
making accusatory remarks without clarifying or verifying the
situation, projecting your feelings onto others.

• *Grandiosity, pretentiousness, pompousness, inflation,
egocentricity*
Examples: showing off, expressing mistrust towards other people,
refusing to delegate, taking losing personally, needing to be the
centre of attention at all times, not listening to or hearing others,
talking over other people's heads, expecting to resolve problems
in your own time-scale, having an inflated view of yourself and
reality, paranoia, addiction to drama.

• *Unpredictability, erraticness, volatility, impulsiveness,
recklessness, inconsistency, unreliability, dangerousness*
Examples: blowing hot and cold, indulging in angry outbursts that
are disproportionate to events, attacking indiscriminately,
dispensing punishment at random ('just to show who is in
charge'), hurting people ('just for the hell of it'), using alcohol and
drugs knowing that they are emotionally destabilising, engaging in
illogical arguments that don't bring about resolution.

• *Mania, hyperactivity, over-excitedness, frenzy, agitation*
Examples: speaking very fast, walking too fast, working too much
and expecting others to fit in and/or keep up, speeding, over-
spending and chronic debt (especially when this deprives others),
doing things too quickly (making mistakes that others have to fix
for you), never being satisfied.

• *Selfishness, unconcern, lack of empathy*
Examples: ignoring other people's needs, not responding to

requests for help, stonewalling, queue-jumping, cutting in when driving.

• *Vengefulness, lack of forgiveness, vindictiveness, bitterness, mercilessness, cold-heartedness, rigidity*
Examples: being over-punitive, holding on to a grudge, refusing to forgive and forget, bringing up wounds from the past, acting with the intention of hurting someone, acting out of spite, refusing to acknowledge someone else's point of view.

EXERCISE
HOW AGGRESSIVE
ARE YOU?

Please be aware that this exercise may bring up some emotional material as you reflect on your behaviour. You may want to have an anger buddy present to encourage you and/or share your insights. Have your journal on hand to make notes about your feelings and insights. This will enable you to review them at a later stage and get a good view of how far you have come.

•

Look back at the bulleted headings above. Now think about your own life. For each heading write down any instances you can think of when you used these particular aggressive behaviours.

•

Once you have completed your list, show it to your anger buddy and discuss your feelings with them. Be open to getting honest feedback from them.

•

Show the list to your family and friends to see whether they agree or disagree with you. They may have noticed a few behaviours that you have left out which need to be included. (See Chapter Seven for guidance on fielding feedback.)

— ⚡ —

Assertiveness – healthy aggression

Participants in my groups are often surprised when I raise the topic of healthy aggression. Many of them can't see how aggression can ever be considered healthy.

The way I look at it, anger can be used in a 'clean' or an 'unclean' way. When anger is designed to hurt others, then it's unclean. This type of anger usually also has some kind of history behind it relating to a hidden trauma or unfinished business from your past. Clean anger, on the other hand, allows us to express our opinions and to get our point across without abusing anyone or anything. Healthy aggression is about assertiveness. It means identifying our needs and making sure they are met, without hurting anyone in any way. This is an art and it takes practice to achieve. Healthy aggression is also an extremely effective way of bringing closure to old hurts and resentments and their associated traumas. Assertive behaviours include the following:

• *Directness, openness, being up-front, honesty, clarity*
Examples: being clear and direct, not beating round the bush, owning up to dysfunctional behaviour, using non-hostile and non-aggressive body language, saying what you mean (and meaning what you say), expressing feelings clearly to others, explaining

how you feel and not what other people think you should feel,
using 'I' statements in conversation.

• *Honour, morality, principle, fairness, discretion, ethics, justice*
Examples: being clear about the legitimate moral basis for your
anger; being willing to resolve the issue in a mature fashion; not
resorting to manipulation or blackmail tactics; not abusing your
position of power or authority; taking responsibility for your
thoughts, feelings, behaviour and actions.

• *Focus, concentration, engagement*
Examples: sticking to the facts and issues concerned; not
confusing the issue with irrelevant information and material; not
bringing up past issues; exploring possibilities for resolution and
closure; staying in the present moment; being open-hearted; being
receptive to feedback, however painful.

• *Persistence, constancy, determination*
Examples: repeating your feelings and the relevant issues over
and over again, being clear about your emotional boundaries,
standing your ground, staying with the issues at hand until they
are sorted out.

• *Courage, bravery, daring, guts, boldness, audacity,
intentionality*
Examples: being willing to take calculated risks, being able to
endure frustrations and emotional discomfort, not being overly
attached to being liked or to outcomes, remaining calm and adult
throughout, taking a lead, being unafraid of other people's anger,
not taking anything personally, being committed to resolution and
relationships no matter what.

• *Passion, enthusiasm, eagerness, keenness, adoration, lovingness*

Examples: being able to express feelings through your body (raising your voice where appropriate) while still being responsive to the needs of others; being open (even when feeling uncomfortable), caring, able to look at the bigger picture; respecting the other person's experience; being sensitive to the consequences of your actions and those of others.

• *Creativity, imagination, originality, resourcefulness, focus on solutions, innovation*

Examples: being able to think quickly and on your feet, having resources of wit and/or humour, always looking for a solution and being creative in negotiating, being non-defeatist, being optimistic, perceiving every obstacle as an opportunity for change and growth, being open to learning and discovering.

• *Empathy, kindness, compassion, forgiveness, concern, consideration*

Examples: being able to hear other people's anger and grievances, being able to feel angry while still keeping your heart open, being able to wipe the slate clean once anger has been expressed, being able to admit to your own shortcomings, thinking inclusively rather than exclusively, being sensitive to the limitations of others, being non-judgemental.

HOW ASSERTIVE ARE YOU?

Look back at the bulleted headings above. Now think about your own life experiences. For each heading write down any instances you can think of when you used these particular assertive behaviours.

•

Acknowledge that you are using some of these assertive behaviours and resolve to continue to develop them in your daily life. Being assertive is much healthier than being aggressive or passive-aggressive.

— ⚡ —

The five faces of anger

I regard anger as having five different faces, or characteristics, each finding expression in a particular type of behaviour. Each face is shaped by how we have (or have not) dealt with our own and other people's feelings and experiences. An awareness of these different faces can help to understand how anger is ignited in the first place.

The faces begin to emerge at an early age, as part of our sophisticated ego defence structure. You can look at each different face as a mask, or persona, that we develop to protect ourselves.

Each face works rather well at first – that is, each one offers us protection from things in life we are afraid of or anxious about – but eventually the faces become tired and worn, and they begin to crack. When this happens, instead of helping us to express our feelings of fear, hurt, sadness, shame, and so on, the faces start to inhibit us. They stop us expressing our true feelings in a healthy way. As a result, many of our feelings are transmuted into passive aggression or outright aggressive behaviour. At this stage, the faces of anger start to dominate our personality.

The task is to recognise which face we are wearing, what that face means to us as an individual, and why we have become attached to it and feel we need it in our life. Only then can we begin the process of transforming the various faces of anger so that we can become emotionally healthy again.

1 The caring face of anger

You often hear people say, 'If I didn't care, I wouldn't be angry with you' or 'I am only angry with you because I care'. The expression of our anger can be seen as being in direct proportion to the depth of our caring and passion for life. This includes the desire to protect ourselves, our loved ones, the planet and anything that matters to us.

On the first evening in my group workshops, participants are asked to fill out a stress questionnaire. It is true to say that feelings of injustice tend to rate high on their stress barometers – a very common trigger for anger. People who feel strongly about injustice have a huge capacity for caring, and this brings an enormous amount of meaning to their lives. Hence their reactions to circumstances or events can vary from a little anger to outrage, depending on how strongly they feel about the situation and how much value they attach to it. They are angry because they care rather than being simply indifferent. If they lose this sense of care, they are faced with a crisis of meaning, and they may believe that in order to cease reacting angrily, they will have to cease caring. Therefore the caring face of anger relates to what holds meaning, value and significance.

If a person fears expressing their own anger, they risk becoming depressed. Where there is anger, there is always hope. Where there is repressed anger, there lies the roots of depression, and when there is depression, quite often all hope is often lost. This is well illustrated in work with angry children and young adults. Children who express their anger are easier to work with than children who are so depressed that they cannot express their feelings in a healthy way. Depressed children often have little hope left and are very hard to reach. They tend to be very passive in their interactions at school and can easily become a target for bullying. If this situation persists, it is only a matter of time before these children drop out of school or fail dismally. If you can reach them through continued trust and patience, and educate them in differentiating between the caring face of anger and the isolating self-destructive qualities of repressed anger, then you are generally able to build a bridge and bring them back into the world.

The caring face of anger is also evident when we use our anger as a way of ensuring that our physical and emotional boundaries are not transgressed. Getting angry in these instances suggests that we respect and care for ourselves enough not to let ourselves be manipulated and have our boundaries broken.

Obviously, where a lot of meaning has been attached to an issue, it carries a huge charge. In this situation, it is therefore easy to fall into expressing our anger in unhelpful ways or in ways that undermine our intentions and integrity. Learning to express your anger when you experience injustices towards yourself and others is the first step; learning to express your anger in an appropriate manner is the second. It is easy to become overwhelmed by the intensity of feelings that arise.

Make a list of where the caring face of anger applies in your
life. For example, you may feel angry when someone you
love is unfairly treated by others, or when you see a parent
in a supermarket being cruel and shaming towards their
their young child. In these circumstances our anger may be
healthy – as long as it is expressed in an appropriate way.

$$- \mskip-4mu \frac{}{} \mskip-4mu -$$

2 The self-diminishing face of anger

People who have low self-esteem or who don't value themselves are
excellent at putting themselves down and giving themselves a very
hard time. Being self-diminishing (or self-forgetting) is an effective
way of turning our anger inwards. It's a passive-aggressive act
directed at ourselves and is a means of keeping ourselves small and
insignificant in the world. As a result of continuously minimising our
own experiences, however, we begin to feel resentment. Others start
to bear the brunt of our built-up aggression, anger and hostility, and
this has a detrimental affect on our personal and professional relationships.

The self-diminishing face of anger has an in-built defence
mechanism that, once activated, creates a self-fulfilling prophecy:
'I will reject myself before you reject me.' People who adopt this face
have learned to cope with their own self-hatred and find it preferable
to the kind of pain they fear they would suffer at the hands of other
people.

The core issue to address with this face is how to identify and
meet our own primary needs – the basic requirement we human

beings have for love, comfort, reassurance and support. (For more on primary needs see Chapter Two.) Part of the process of overcoming self-diminishing anger is commiting yourself to identifying what your needs are and then taking responsibility for getting them met. Once you are able to do this, you will naturally find that your need to self-sabotage or self-destruct will slowly dissolve. It takes practice, but it is possible and it does work.

In the past, when I found myself in uncomfortable situations I often noticed that I felt scared. I would usually not stick up for myself, even though a voice inside my head was telling me, 'Michael, say something, do something! Don't let this person get away with this sort of insensitive behaviour.' The problem was that I wanted the other person to see me as nice, caring and emotionally sorted, so I repressed my feeling of anger. And in so doing, I diminished myself. I was also generally unwilling to say how I really felt, in case I upset the other person or hurt their feelings. In effect, this meant that it was OK for me to feel hurt but it was not OK for them to feel hurt as a result of me sharing my feelings. By keeping my feelings inside, I was not being true to myself.

EXERCISE
THE SELF-DIMINISHING FACE OF ANGER

Look back at the examples above of the ways in which I used to diminish myself. Now make a list of how you diminish or forget yourself and how this impacts on and affects others.

— ⚡ —

3 The numb face of anger

Many of us use anger as a way of numbing ourselves. Expressions of hostility and anger become a smokescreen obscuring other distressing feelings such as sadness, fear, hurt and shame. Offloading our anger onto others feels safer than expressing and communicating the full range and complexity of our feelings. People who wear this face need to remember that in fact the more angry they become, the more emotionally impotent, vulnerable and powerless they end up feeling – exactly what they are trying to avoid.

If you wear this face of anger, it is important to find a way of sitting with the discomfort of your own emotional pain and containing your anger. You need to recognise that habitually dumping your anger on someone else serves only to numb you and cause others confusion and pain. Begin the process of finding a healthy and meaningful way to express the full range of all your feelings. Allow yourself really to feel your hurt, fear, sadness and shame, and express these feelings to others without self-recrimination. People will respect and value you more, and you will gain self-respect and be much happier.

EXERCISE
THE NUMB FACE OF ANGER

Identify instances when you have used anger to avoid feeling another emotion. We may do this, for example, by moaning and groaning continuously; by finding fault with others; or by hyping ourselves up until we explode under the effects of adrenalin, enjoying the euphoria of the release. Acknowledge how your behaviour impacted on and affected others.

— ⚡ —

4 The unrealistic face of anger

The unrealistic face of anger is based as a response to expectations of how *I should be*, how the world *should be* and how others *should* behave. By adopting it we give ourselves permission – and justification – for blowing our top. We have every reason for punishing others, or so we believe. Unrealistic expectations create conflict and misery, and entertaining them can become a very dangerous game to play. While you're judging others for not getting it 'right' or being 'good enough', you avoid having to look at your own imperfections, shortcomings and shadow projections (more about this in Chapters Two and Five).

Many of us impose our ideals onto others as a way of feeling superior; however, this is merely a cover-up for deep feelings of inferiority – a way of hiding the fact that we feel unconfident. In order to feel good about ourselves, we have to put others down by judging and criticising them when they fail to meet our unrealistic expectations. We may experience a profound sense of entitlement or specialness, feeling that the world owes us something we don't have to work for.

A great deal of anger is motivated by an inability to accept the world the way it is. However, anger won't change the world. By continuously expressing unrealistic anger, we just make a gigantic hole for ourselves. And the more we use anger to get us out of the hole, the deeper the hole gets.

In order to begin emerging from the hole, we need to hear the feedback that others have to give to us, even if it is difficult to hear. We have to understand that other people are not the enemy; the enemy lies deep within. (We will explore this further in Chapter Two.) We must make it a priority to recognise that when we judge and criticise others, we are trying – ineffectively – to feel better about ourselves. There are far more effective ways of esteeming ourselves. Once we discover this, our unrealistic expectations of others will diminish, including the constant need to prove ourselves.

EXERCISE
THE UNREALISTIC FACE OF ANGER

Make a list of all the unrealistic expectations you have of yourself.

•

Now do the same for the unrealistic expecations you have of others. If you find this difficult, look at the judgements you make about others; they often contain an expectation.

•

Now consider what effect this behaviour has on those close to you. Write down your reflections in your journal.

— ⚡ —

5 The addictive face of anger

When we are wearing this face, we turn to an addictive substance or behaviour in order to avoid experiencing our anger. This face reflects the extraordinary length to which we will go in order to avoid our anger.

At some time or other, all of us experience some form of emotional pain within the context of the family; whether this pain is acknowledged and expressed within the family will determine the mental health of each individual and of the family system. The lack of expression or communication of painful feelings forces them deep into the unconscious, whereby they may manifest as some form of addictive or compulsive disorder. This enables the psyche to endure the psychological pain of repression.

Addictions serve to anaesthetise us. They give us an instant feel-good sensation. Eventually, however, we still have to face not just our original trauma but also shame and remorse as a result of the effect that our behaviour has had on ourselves and others. When this, too, is too painful to feel, we then return to the addiction to minimise our negative feelings – and so the cycle perpetuates itself.

Addictive anger manifests through four main avoidance behaviours.

Drugs of choice

I am using 'drugs' here in a loose sense, to indicate not only substances such as drugs and alcohol but also behaviours such as sex, intensity, work, drama, adrenaline, gambling, food, shopping and so on – in other words, anything that is used inappropriately to alleviate pain and suffering.

A word about addiction to alcohol. Drinking results in one of two consequences. The first, of course, is the drowning out of all pain – indeed, of all feeling. The second, paradoxically, is that under the influence of alcohol the very thing we are trying to repress often raises its ugly head. Like me, you have probably come across people who appear as quiet as a doormouse until they begin to drink – when their destructive anger explodes. It may be the aftermath of a drinking bout that forces such a person to acknowledge that they have an anger management problem, as they witness the destruction they have left behind. If you have an addiction to alcohol, it will be necessary for you to address your drinking habits before you start working on anger management.

I always suggest that people with an alcohol or drug addiction see a specialist in addiction counselling or join one of the many local AA (Alcoholics Anonymous) or NA (Narcotics Anonymous) groups. You will find contact details for these organisations on page 261.

Religion

Karl Marx famously said, 'Religion is the opiate of the masses.' While religion can be an influence for personal and communal good, there are those of us who use it as an emotional bypass, giving over the responsibility for how we lead our lives to God. This means, in essence, that we never have to grow up. God the father is there to take care of us and wipe our sins away. If we never grow up emotionally, we remain in a passive state. Religion becomes a powerful drug that enables us to avoid feelings of despair, pain and suffering.

Yet if we do not take responsibility for our lives – which includes taking responsibility for our behaviour, thoughts, actions and feelings – we are not fulfilling our promise as human beings. God wants us to be fully coherent and in charge of our own life. One of the greatest gifts we can give God is to take up this challenge.

Spiritual materialism (the new age)

Since the early 1960s, many people in the Western world have come to believe that in order to transcend life's banalities and perceived meaninglessness, they have had to journey inwards, towards the true 'final frontier'. On the whole this movement has been a positive vehicle for self-realisation (and for the welfare of the planet), yet it is possible to use new-age spirituality as a means of avoiding our deeper, darker sides. The piecemeal importation of Eastern and/or tribal spiritual traditions, practices and rituals has sometimes created scope for individuals to hide from feeling, owning, expressing and communicating their painful 'negative' feelings.

An example of this kind of avoidant behaviour might be: 'Every time I get angry or someone is angry with me, I shroud myself in white light, hold my favourite crystal in my pocket and chant 'om' to protect me from the negative energy that others project onto me.' This is all fine if you have a truly healthy relationship with your own and other people's anger. However, it is extremely unhealthy when you are looking to defend yourself against feeling your own feelings. Spiritual materialism may, in the short term, be a security blanket in the face of our own internal dark forces, but in the end we all have to face our demons. Anger cannot be avoided, however hard we try and however many incense sticks we burn. We still have to do our anger work!

Intellectualism

Intellectualism is frequently the addiction of choice for those who are mind-identified. Intellectualisers have little or no awareness of their feelings, body or spirit. They live in their heads and rationalise everything that happens to them. They tend to bury their feelings beneath words and are often criticised for being emotionally unreachable or crippled. They are often dissociated from their bodies, living from their neck up.

Intellectualisers believe that they can control and outsmart their own feelings. In reality, however, life just needs to throw them a little curve ball and they completely fall apart emotionally. It may be only then that they begin to accept the need to develop a meaningful relationship with their feelings in order to function fully in the world.

EXERCISE
ADDICTIVE ANGER

Identify which behaviour you use by asking others to give you feedback. Try to acknowledge what they say, rather than just seeing their opinions as negative. Experience yourself as others see you.

•

Look at how this behaviour manifests and record your reflections in your journal.

•

Consider the effect addictive anger has on you and others.
Once again, record your reflections in your journal.

— ϟ —

The angry brain

Anger has a relationship to history and to a situation, but it is also
a biological experience – a primitive biochemical response in our
brains. In order to understand why the brain functions as it does in
confrontational situations, we need to familiarise ourselves with
some of its territory.

The brain has three significant and easily distinguishable
components. For this reason it is often referred to as 'the triune
brain' ('triune' meaning 'in three parts'). Each component has a role
to play in keeping us alive and safe and is a product of our evolu-
tionary development as human beings.

Originally, each component of the brain evolved to function as a
single entity, and therefore each has distinctive characteristics and
abilities. For fully evolved human beings, however, it is essential that
all three brains work together, especially in situations where there
is high arousal, uncertainty or danger. Each brain is inextricably
linked with the others. All three communicate with one another and
prepare the body for its emotional and/or physical response.

Let's now look at the three components of the human brain.

The reptilian brain

- 700 million years old – oldest part of the brain
- Governs survival and territorial instincts and reflexes
- Maintains basic involuntary bodily functions, for example
  body temperature, heart rate, respiration and reflexes

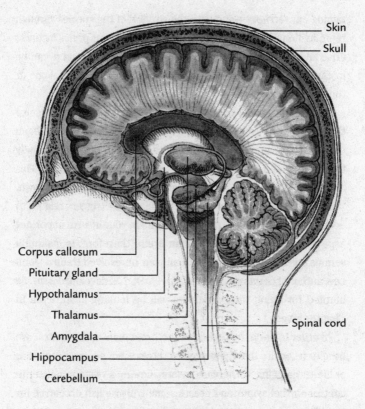

Skin
Skull

Corpus callosum
Pituitary gland
Hypothalamus
Thalamus
Amygdala
Hippocampus
Cerebellum

Spinal cord

Cross section of the brain

* Is linked to the autonomic nervous system, which governs our muscular and organ responses to stress and relaxation, including sexual arousal and the hyper-arousal of the fight, flight or freeze mechanism

The reptilian brain is the 'original' brain that helped our species to survive in the swamps when we were still amphibian. It is concerned with individual survival – with finding food and protecting and maintaining our territory – and with the survival of the species through reproduction. It houses the limbic system, where our primal instincts arise and involuntary body functions are regulated, and it can be instantaneously triggered without any conscious reason, logic or thought.

It is our reptilian brain that initially responds when we perceive that a physical, emotional or psychological boundary has been crossed, for example by increasing the heart rate, raising the body temperature and sending adrenalin coursing through the body. This reaction can happen in a split second, and it can lead to meltdown.

The reptilian brain can also be stimulated by triggers related to deep-seated unresolved traumatic events in your life. An important aspect of controlling the reptilian brain, therefore, is making a serious commitment to deal with all your unresolved trauma. John Lee, author of *Growing Yourself Up Again*, has developed a simple method for doing this, which we will be looking at in detail in Chapter Five.

In order to bring the reptilian brain's reactions under control, we need to recognise that the perceived threat is not necessarily serious or life-threatening – otherwise we are allowing a swamp-monster to control our behaviour and create some truly hellish outcomes for ourselves. Taking control of the reptilian brain is not easy. Let's face it: we're up against 700 million years' worth of pure primal energy. We need every ounce of awareness, concentration and discipline we can muster to control the surge of raw adrenaline and cortisol pumping through our veins. Nevertheless, it's your responsibility to contain your reactions – and you know how much not doing this has cost you already, otherwise you wouldn't be reading this book. In order to do this, you need to enlist the help of your mammalian and your new brain.

The mammalian brain

- 70 million years old – second part of the brain to evolve
- Involved with curiosity, emotion, nurturing, altruism and social structures
- Attached to the limbic system and consists of the hippocampus and the amygdala, the two lobes on either side of the brain
- Associated with the thalamus, which flanks the limbic system and acts as the relay centre for sensory information coming from the body on its way to the cortex

The mammalian brain evolved, of course, as amphibians evolved into mammals, and it relates to much mammalian behaviour and brain function, such as the ability to function within a group and to nurture young (neither of which are reptilian behaviours). Emotion and curiosity help mammals to bond and flourish. They learn from each other and sometimes hunt together and share their kill.

The mammalian brain works in conjunction with the reptilian brain. Attached to the limbic system are two lobes called the hippocampus and the amygdala. The amygdala processes and stores emotions, including our reactions to emotionally charged events. The hippocampus processes the data surrounding an event and puts it in its time frame or sequence. The thalamus is also part of this system, its two parts flanking the limbic system. It acts as the relay centre for sensory information coming from the body on its way to the cortex.

Being the storehouse for emotional memories and feelings, the mammalian brain acts like a sentinel to our inner landscape. It specialises in emotional matters. It accesses and assimilates significant interactions in our daily lives – in a matter of seconds. It then translates these incidents into a range of emotional responses, again in only seconds. With the aid of the reptilian brain it constantly looks out for danger and, if it registers any, the reptilian brain activates the fight, flight or freeze mechanism, putting us in a state of high alert.

To the strong physiological responses of the reptilian brain, the mammalian brain adds highly charged emotions. Like many of us, you may have a memory of a traumatic event that is full of emotion – and perhaps also physical sensation – but that lacks the context of time or place. This is because in a highly stressful situation the mammalian brain can react to the present as if it were the past. The reason for this is that when stress levels are high, prolonged secretion of cortisol suppresses the activity of the hippocampus (which gives data around events - a context of time and sequence). The amygdalla (which processes emotional experiences) remains unaffected by cortisol and therefore the distressing memories remain intense.

These strong emotional memories often remain stored within us, and can easily become a trigger for over-reaction in our present lives. For example, a simple failure in work may trigger a deep sense of shame related to when we were nine years old and our father punished us for not passing a maths test. As a result, we become over-sensitive to our boss's feedback and respond with dispropor-tionate emotion. This phenomenon has been described by Daniel Goleman in his well-known book *Emotional Intelligence*. He calls it emotional hijacking. Importantly, this emotional response occurs almost instantly, moments before the new brain has had a chance to grasp what is occurring and decide on a rational basis what the best course of action might be.

The new brain

* 100 thousand years old – newest part of the brain

* Can solve problems and predict consequences of present behaviour
* Deals with language and symbols
* Enables self-awareness

The new brain, or cerebral cortex, has evolved most recently and makes it possible for higher-brain functions such as learning, thinking, reasoning, imagining, communicating, problem-solving, using language and understanding. It is the strategic command centre that steps in after the reptilian and emotional brains to control our reactions and responses to potentially volatile situations. When we find ourselves being affected by our own or another's behaviour, by an unwelcome event or by a difficult situation, the new brain enables us to think through the consequences carefully and respond from a considered viewpoint. Thus it enables us to become emotionally intelligent and thereby manage our anger, aggression and hostility, ensuring that we are not held to ransom by either of the two older brains.

In an ideal situation the various parts of the brain are perfect partners, working in cooperation with one another. The reptilian and mammalian brains alert the new brain, and the new brain considers all the angles before creating a strategic, well-thought-out action plan. All too often, however, the reptilian and mammalian overpower the new brain, thus impairing our ability to think and reason effectively. Our fear immobilises us, and our anger causes us to lash out. It is as if the two older brains create neural static, thus sabotaging the new brain. This is why we complain that we 'can't think straight' when we are upset.

These emotional circuits and the automatic reactions that they set in chain are sculpted by past experiences, particularly those of childhood. This will be explained in more detail in Chapter Five.

The FLOW process

The FLOW process is a simple safety mechanism that I have created to prevent the new brain being overwhelmed by the two older brains. When you are in a situation where you are emotionally triggered, use the following four tactics.

F stands for **focus**

Plant your feet firmly on the ground and breathe slowly and deeply into your belly. Make each inhalation last for seven seconds and each exhalation last for eleven seconds. Fix all your attention on the simple act of breathing air in and breathing air out, so that you remain present. Focus your energy in your belly – this will help to bring you back to your body. Above all else, keep breathing slowly and steadily, without hyper-ventilating.

L stands for **listen** and **learn**

Concentrating on what the other person is saying keeps you present and also enables you to learn what they really feel. Make every effort to fully understand what the other person is saying or doing.

O stands for **objectivity**

Stop, think and take a look at the big picture. Do your best to empathise and not take what the other person is saying personally. (As soon as you start to take it personally, you lose all sense of objectivity about the situation.)

W stands for **wait**

In the heat of the moment it is vital to contain your feelings. Sit in your discomfort and wait until you can respond appropriately without any aggression or resentment. It always pays to wait.

Before you move on to the next chapter, take a moment to reflect on what you have learnt from Chapter One. What stands out? Have certain parts of the chapter spoken to you more clearly than others? Which have been the hardest to accept? (It may well be that it's these you most need to pay attention to.)

Most important of all, take a moment now to thank yourself for reading this far and for putting in the time and effort to make positive changes in your life. You're doing really well. Keep up the good work!

CHAPTER 2
Why We Get Angry

Anger is a response to a perceived threat – past, present or future.

—Roger Koester

This chapter of the book will help you to discover and understand what the key triggers are for your anger. We will be delving further into the issues that can trigger anger and looking at how some people come to rely on their anger as a vital part of themselves. We will also be considering how anger can be used as a defence mechanism and how anger relates to our primary needs as human beings.

Values, core beliefs and goals

Anger informs us that something is not quite right. Our primary instincts become activated and then our fight, flight or freeze mechanism is awakened – and all hell can break loose! This may be over what seems to be the most trivial of incidents – and perhaps on the surface it is. When we scratch the surface, however, no incident is trivial. There is always an underlying trigger for our anger.

Beneath our anger is the sense that our values, core beliefs (negative or positive) or goals are being threatened and invalidated in some way – even though we are often unable to clearly define or articulate the nature of this perceived threat. Let's look in more detail at what we mean by values, core beliefs and goals.

• *Values*
The accepted principles or standards of an individual or a group. For example: honesty, caring, integrity and reliability.

• *Core beliefs*
What the individual or group mind holds to be true or real, often underpinned by an emotional or spiritual sense of certainty. For example: 'The family is very important', 'Generosity is a virtue', 'The earth needs to be cared for and protected', 'Elders should be respected'.

• *Goals*
Objectives that an individual or group wants to achieve. For example: a directorship, health and fitness, the ability to care and provide for one's family, enough money to go on holiday once a year.

Our values, core beliefs and goals usually evoke strong feelings, and it is therefore important to be aware of whether our anger around them is in proportion to the event or not. Should any of them be transgressed in any way our anger will quickly rise to the surface and we may find ourselves behaving in infantile ways. Our reaction will be an exaggerated form of either aggression or passive aggression.

Negative core beliefs

In almost all instances where we become emotionally regressed, the underlying motive for our response is a negative core belief – in other words, a belief that the core of who we are is damaged or bad. Examples of negative core beliefs might be:

* I am a bad person
* I am a mistake
* However hard I try, I just cannot get it right
* I am unlovable
* I am dirty
* I am stupid
* No one loves me
* I am evil
* I am a monster

Negative core beliefs exist in our unconscious and are associated with a historical traumatic event. They manifest as our internal judge and critic, and their function is to protect others from who we believe we truly are. Their negative internal dialogue rules our inner lives like a psychic mafia, droning on about how bad we are and how if others knew us they would be horrified by what we think and feel. They encourage us to deceive ourselves, reject ourselves and abandon ourselves.

These are the parts of ourselves that we hide, deny and repress, that we are afraid to look at or are ashamed of. Ironically, it is precisely these aspects that we see reflected in others and that we react to. Dr Carl Jung has coined the term 'shadow' to refer to negative core beliefs – we will be discussing the shadow in more detail on pages 72–78 and 188–94.

EXERCISE
DISCOVER YOUR ANGER ACTIVATORS

Make a list of of six personal values that you hold to be important – for example:

1 I am an honest person.

2 I am a caring person.

3 I respect others, and they respect me.

4 I attempt to behave with integrity towards my self and others at all times.

5 I expect people to hold me accountable when I don't behave with integrity.

6 I take responsibility for my own emotional wellbeing.

•

Make a list of six goals you wish to achieve – for example:

1 To succeed in my work.

2 To be respected by my family.

3 To drive across America on a motorcycle.

4 To make and sell my sculptures.

5 To complete a doctorate on male psychology.

6 To die with dignity and peacefully.

•

Make a list of six negative core beliefs that you hold about yourself – for example:

1 I am unlovable.

2 I am thick.

3 People don't really trust me.

4 People only love me for what I do.

5 I am not a good, caring person.

6   I am selfish.

•

Make a list of six shadows that operate in your life – for example:

1   I don't trust other people and am not to be trusted.

2   I am a slob.

3   I should never let go of control.

4   I don't really deserve happiness.

5   If you betray me, I will hurt you.

6   I often lie to myself and others.

•

Look at your examples and consider that when our values, goals, negative core belief and shadows come into play, our anger is often triggered. Next time you find yourself getting angry, stop and ask yourself if any of these factors is involved. Once you are able to ask yourself these questions, you can begin to make choices about your reactions, which is much healthier than lashing out automatically.

$$- \not\! 4 -$$

How our behaviour affects and triggers others

Although we may not be aware of it, our own actions activate a series of triggers in our relationships with others. And once they are triggered, we may be triggered to react to their reaction, thus setting in chain a negative spiral of reactions.

Often, we are blissfully unaware of how our behaviour appears to other people, failing to recognise that our behaviour evokes disrespect or resentment. A client recently came to see me after a series of seriously abusive outbursts that culminated in his wife leaving him. With my help, he decided to ask everyone he was close to how they experienced his behaviour. He asked them to be very honest with him, which they were. To his amazement, their image of him was very different from the way he perceived himself. True, they recognised positive aspects of his character, but they also saw much of his behaviour in a very negative light. He, on the other hand, saw himself only in a positive light.

EXERCISE
HOW OTHERS SEE ME

Since many of us fail to recognise the impact we have on those around us, it is useful to ask others how they see us. Choose several people to do this exercise with – family members, close friends and colleagues. Opt for those you can trust to be honest.

•

Ask each friend, colleague or relation about the aspects of yourself that get in the way of you having healthy relationships with others. Reassure them that you want to hear the truth. Make a note of what they say, being as accurate as you can and resisting the urge to change the significance of their words.

•

Share your notes with an anger buddy or another person you can trust and listen to their feedback.

— ⚡ —

The four causes of anger

There are four causes that set the stage for an angry response. They are:

* Failure to achieve a personal goal – for example arriving late for a meeting, failing an exam, losing a job.
* Invasion of a personal boundary – for example someone entering your room or personal space without permission, being touched without permission, being spoken too disrespectfully.
* Self-defence anger – for example feeling the constant need to defend yourself because you are 'not intelligent enough' to do your job. I have found that people who are shame-based use anger as a way of deflecting their toxic feelings of shame. (More about this on page 177.)
* Shadow projection– for example you are ashamed of your gluttony and make a point of always eating sparely; then you encounter someone greedily attacking a four-course dinner. Or you are embarrassed about your working-class origins and try to conceal them; then you meet someone who is proud to be a plumber's son.

EXERCISE
THE CAUSES OF YOUR ANGER

Take about five minutes to think of at least two situations in which you became angry because of failure to achieve a personal goal. Make notes about these incidents. For example, 'Last week I lost my car keys and was late for a supervision meeting.'

·

Take about five minutes to think of at least two situations in which you became angry because of an invasion of your personal boundaries. Make notes about these incidents. For example, 'My mum cleaned up my desk yesterday and I couldn't find my stuff.'

•

Take about five minutes to think about situations in which a chip on your shoulder or something you are ashamed about was activated. Make notes about these incidents. For example, 'When Dave started talking about computers again, I thought how much I hate nerds.'

•

Take about five minutes to think of at least two situations in which you became angry because one of your shadows was mirrored by someone else. Make notes about these incidents. For example, 'Last night I met someone who was loud and bossy and I wanted to put them down and judge them.'

— ⚡ —

Becoming conscious

Anger management is all about being conscious of background uncertainties, which I call 'white noise'. It's about recognising your triggers and the triggers of others around you. Once you have achieved this task, you no longer have to be at the mercy of your own infantile behaviour or that of others.

Bear in mind that when you are stressed out or in the state known in addiction recovery as HALT (Hungry, Angry, Lonely and Tired), you will tend to be over-sensitive and reactive and are more likely to act in an emotionally regressive way. Remind yourself that you can always walk away from the combat zone, leaving the fight until another day. You may also want to apply the eight golden rules of anger-management, which we will be talking about in Chapter Seven.

Developing a sensitivity to other people's moods and behaviours will allow you to notice when they may be becoming prickly. At this point it is important not to take what they are saying or doing personally. Recognise that their prickliness is their way of projecting – or off-loading – their negative feelings onto you. They are doing this in order to cope, and it is neither good nor bad. Being aware of this will help you to avoid getting drawn into a drama cycle.

Being able to recognise these signals is about staying present to events and situations that are going on around us all the time. In order to do this, we deliberately slow down our internal experiences in order to have the time to notice feelings, thoughts, responses and reactions moment by moment and make mature choices about how best to act – or not act – on them.

There are numerous ways of doing this, and many books have been written on the subject. One method is to write down in your journal what you are feeling and how these feelings are affecting you spiritually, psychologically and physically. Also notice your internal dialogue, writing this down too. Writing in your journal brings you and your internal processes into the present.

You might also consider meditating. Close your eyes, relax, focus on your breath and then just notice your thoughts and feelings. Remember, all you need to do is notice. By allowing yourself to do this, you may find that you can relax into the situation you find yourself in. Taking a class in meditation can be very useful in managing your anger and reducing your stress levels. See also the FLOW process on page 52.

The choices that we make moment to moment affect how we live. I know for a fact that the choices I used to make (and which I wasn't even aware I was making) were an effort to avoid psychic and emotional pain. Because I was acting without self-awareness, every act that I intended to increase the amount of pleasure and joy in my life, just dug my hole of despair a little deeper. Nothing I did was guided by conscious choice. Instead, I was driven by low self-esteem. I wanted people to like me, to love me and to take care of me – and to collude in my destructive behaviour, allowing me the opportunity to manipulate them. So I made sure that I attracted those kinds of people into my life. This caused me further unhappiness, resentment and discontent.

The choices we make when we say yes or no are vital to our wellbeing, and we need to be clear about what drives them. It is therefore vital that we remain conscious so that we can live life fully, unadulterated by constant pain and self-destruction. The following poem, by William Stafford, illustrates this point.

A Ritual to Read to Each Other

If you don't know the kind of person I am
and I don't know the kind of person you are
a pattern that others made may prevail in the world
and following the wrong god home we may miss our star.

For there is many a small betrayal in the mind,
a shrug that lets the fragile sequence break
sending with shouts the horrible errors of childhood
storming out to play through the broken dyke.

And as elephants parade holding each elephant's tail,
but if one wanders the circus won't find the park,
I call it cruel and maybe the root of all cruelty
to know what occurs but not to recognise the fact.

> For it is important that awake people be awake,
> or a breaking line may discourage them back to sleep;
> the signals we give – yes or no, or maybe –
> should be clear: the darkness around us is deep.

If you would like to read more about the significance of living in the moment, try reading *The Power of Now* by Eckhart Tolle. The book discusses the importance of becoming present to making healthy choices rather than self-destructive ones, which are usually driven by our own pain and distress.

Making conscious adult choices in the moment on how best to deal with the situations you find yourself in can be powerfully transformative. Your self-esteem will increase and you will become increasingly clear about what you need, what you want and how you feel about yourself and others. This is a significant step towards beating anger.

Defining ourselves through our anger

A few years ago, I was facilitating a men's group that had been running for over ten years. An experienced member of the group spoke about how some of us come to define ourselves through our anger. We explored how our use of anger can give us form, definition and shape, until eventually we find that combat is the only way we can interact with others. We may fear that if we let go of our anger, we will somehow lose our 'edge', or some other facet of our character that we value in some way – even if more often than not it leads us into trouble.

I was inspired by this concept and began to think about how we all in some way define ourselves through different types of behaviour. The more I thought about it, the more I realised how much my own self-perception was guided by my choice of anger –

and for the first time I started to find the language to describe this process.

I began to speak to friends and family about how I had been using my anger as an 'acid test' for their love – that is, if I could push against them without them buckling, they must love me. I had always seen this as healthy and pragmatic. I never considered that it could be dysfunctional and even abusive. To me it seemed like a very effective way of sorting friend from foe. I would use provocative behaviour, language or ideas every time I met a stranger as a way to test their reactions and responses to me. If they over-reacted, I believed that they were not to be trusted. This was how I defined my relationships, by constantly testing others. (We will be looking in more detail at this anger style, known as the winder-upper in Chapter Four).

Another common way in which we define ourselves through our anger is by using it to mark our personal boundaries. When we do not know how to define our boundaries for ourselves, we persistently push against other people so that they are forced to set up the boundary for us. When they challenge us, we experience the boundary, even though our response may be to fly off the handle.

Why is it that some of us need to define ourselves through our anger? The easy answer, of course, is that we are generally not even aware that this is happening; it is totally unconscious behaviour and has probably been learned from a primary carer or older sibling or in the school playground. Some who later use this strategy may have been bullies in childhood. The bully defines himself by intimidating those whom secretly he feels threatened by (this is the shadow being played out again). Later in life this intimidation is translated into challenging and provocative behaviour designed to test the limits of others.

If you recognise in yourself any of the behavours mentioned in this section, try the following exercise.

EXERCISE
DEFINING YOURSELF
THROUGH ANGER

Write down examples of the kind of behaviour you use.

Ask yourself the following questions:

- How does it serve me to behave like this? What do I gain?

- Why do I feel the need to test others' love for me?

- Who in my family behaved the same way?

- What do I need to do in order to refrain from using this self-sabotaging behaviour?

Anger as a defence mechanism

I once asked an anger management group, 'If anger is a defence, what is it a defence against?' The group responded, 'A defence against our own pain, hurt, fear and shame.' I was struck by the way that the group identified how anger can so easily cover up much deeper feelings. In fact, I would go as far as to say that all inappropriate anger is used as a defence mechanism against some form of pain.

Defence mechanisms protect us from overwhelming feelings by repressing painful thoughts or emotions until such time as our ego is strong enough to deal with them. They may protect against anger, fear, sadness, hurt, shame, depression, greed, envy, competitiveness, love, desire, admiration, dependency, selfishness, grandiosity, helplessness and many other feelings. In the meantime these unconscious thoughts or feelings are expressed in indirect or disguised forms. Defence mechanisms come into operation whenever a feared or actual loss begins to arouse our anxiety. Their primary functions are:

* To minimise anxiety
* To protect the ego
* To repress feelings that would cause us emotional discomfort and pain

Defence mechanisms are used to hide a variety of memories or thoughts. There is a large number of different defence mechanisms, many of which are only subtly different from one other. (Indeed, just about anything can become a defence mechanism if it is used to conceal what we are really feeling.) We all use these mechanisms from time to time, and each of us tends to favour certain ones, making them a central part of our style and character. We may choose different defence mechanisms at different times in our life. The following are a few examples. See if you recognise the ones you use:

* Denial: you completely reject the thought or feeling – for example 'I'm not an angry person.'
* Suppression: you are vaguely aware of the thought or feeling but attempt to hide it – for example 'I'm going to try to be nice to him.'
* Reaction formation: you turn the feeling into its opposite – for example 'I don't want to hurt you; I love you.'
* Projection: you think someone else has your thought or feeling – for example 'My boss really hates me.'
* Displacement: you redirect your feelings to another target – for example 'I don't have an anger problem as such, but I do get angry when I'm driving.'
* Rationalisation: you come up with various explanations to justify the situation (while denying your feelings) – for

example 'He is just in a bad mood; I know he really cares for me.'

* Intellectualisation: you use logic to cut off a situation's emotional charge (a form of rationalisation) – 'This situation reminds me of how Nietzsche said that anger is ontological despair.'

* Isolation of affect: you 'think' the feeling but don't really feel it – for example 'I guess I'm angry with him, sort of.'

* Isolation: you avoid the person or issue you have a problem with – for example 'She does not really like me anyway.'

* Undoing: you try to reverse or undo your feeling by doing something that indicates the opposite feeling. This can take the form of apologising for the feeling you find unacceptable within yourself or atoning for and thus counteracting desires and acts that you feel, on some level, are 'immoral' or 'wrong' – for example 'I think I'll buy her a big bunch of flowers.'

* Regression: you revert to an old, usually immature, behaviour to ventilate your feelings – for example 'Don't tell me to grow up, I am grown up!'

* Sublimation: you redirect the feeling into a socially endorsed activity – for example 'I know what I need right now: a stiff scotch on the rocks.'

* Repression: you find any way you can of preventing the feeling from entering your consciousness – 'I know he's only joking with me.'

* Compensation: you substitute other, less threatening, activities for anger – for example 'It's such fun spending time with you; we must do this more often.'

* Defensive devaluation: you attempt to cover up your true feelings – for example 'It's not always my fault; don't blame me all the time.'

* Withdrawal: you remove yourself either emotional or physically – for example 'I don't care if I get that promotion or not.'
* Turning against the self: you direct your hostile impulses towards yourself instead of expressing anger to the person you are angry with – for example 'I'm so stupid and clumsy.'
* Fantasy: you gratify frustrated desires with imaginary achievement – for example 'I am so proud of myself; I only got angry four times today.'
* Acting out – you reduce the anxiety aroused by forbidden desires by permitting yourself to express them. This can involve introjection, where you take on external values and standards so that you remove the pain of transgressing your own normal standards of behaviour – for example 'I'm applying to join the police force' (when in your heart you are drawn towards being a criminal).
* Emotional insulation: you withdraw into passivity – for example, 'I'm just not going to apply for any more jobs.'

The problem with defence mechanisms is that they replace intimacy and contact. While they may make us feel safe in the short term, in the long term they can become so habitual that they turn into a neurosis. We then face the task of disentangling ourselves from them so that we can be clear about who we really are and what aspects of our behaviour reflect our defence mechanisms.

EXERCISE
IDENTIFY YOUR DEFENCE MECHANISMS

Identifying our key defence mechanisms helps us to become more conscious of what we are really feeling.

•

Read through the list above and identify the defence mechanisms that you use.

•

Make a list of what you do. Be explicit. For example: 'I use anger to control others, this is a defence mechanism.'

•

Next time you find yourself turning to one of your defence mechanisms, pause and consider.

— ⚡ —

Primary needs

Our anger can also be aroused when our primary needs are not met. A primary need is something that is required for our wellbeing or survival (as opposed to a want, which is desired but is not vital to us). When our primary needs are not met, anger, hurt and fear are activated, and our survival instincts become imperative. We are hardwired to feel that in order to survive we must take a strong course of action to protect ourselves. Thus when we respond to the denial of a primary need with anger, underlying this reaction will be feelings of powerlessness, helplessness and fear.

Unfortunately, most of us with an anger management problem are unaware of the relationship of anger to primary needs – although recognising and meeting our own primary needs is a facet of being a fully functioning, emotionally healthy human being ... someone who exudes self-confidence and self-esteem and who knows themselves very well.

Some of the main primary needs are to be:

* Valued
* Safe
* Significant
* Cared for
* Seen
* Heard
* Accepted
* Appreciated
* Acknowledged
* Held
* Touched
* Respected
* Encouraged
* Useful
* A member of the 'tribe' (belong)
* Treated honestly
* Treated fairly
* Trusted
* Loved

See if you can list a few more.

If all of the above primary needs are met, we feel unconditionally loved. If these needs have not been met in childhood, as adults the onus is on us to meet *our own* unmet needs. In order to do so, of course, we need to discover what they are, and this is when anger becomes very useful. Whenever we feel angry (or hurt or afraid) we can be sure that a primary need is not being met, either by ourselves or by others.

EXERCISE
**WHAT ARE YOUR UNMET
PRIMARY NEEDS?**

With the help of the list above, do a little detective work
to discover what your unmet needs are and make a list of
them in your journal. For example: 'I don't feel appreciated
by others', 'I don't feel that I belong' and so on.

•

Consider what you would need to change in your life in
order to get your unmet needs met. Write this down. For
example: 'I need to appreciate myself more and not be
attached to others showing appreciation of me', 'I need to
spend more time with positive, caring people'.

•

Consider whether you can begin the process of either
meeting these needs yourself of asking someone else (a
support person) to meet them for you. Write down your
answers. For example: 'I can reward myself and share my
accomplishments with others', 'I can read more books
about self-esteem and share the content with loved ones'.

$-\frac{4}{7}-$

Shadow projections

Once you become familiar with your primary needs you can begin to
consider your shadow projections (which we have already spoken
about briefly on page 56). Dealing with shadow projections is an
essential part of healing yourself and dealing with your anger. They
occur when another person's behaviour reflects an issue of our own
or an aspect of ourselves that we are embarrassed about or ashamed
by. Instead of owning this part of ourselves and our reaction to it

(which would be too painful) we project our distaste onto someone who mirrors this particular aspect of us.

Whenever a person is defensive and needs to justify themselves continually, shadow material is at work. When our shadow material is stimulated, we will often behave in a way that causes others to experience us as shifty, nervous, irate, impatient, short-tempered and so on.

The most usual shadow projections are dark ones – the qualities in ourselves that we perceive as bad. However, we can also deny, repress and disown our golden shadows – that is, positive attributes that we may, equally, be ashamed of. If, for example, you have a wonderful voice but your parents mocked you when you sang at family gatherings as a child, you may feel a lot of shame about singing. We will be discussing the golden shadow in more detail on page 189.

EXERCISE
IDENTIFY YOUR SHADOW PROJECTIONS

This exercise will help you to familiarise yourself with the concept of shadow projections and see how it translates into your life. Answer the following questions.

- Do you ever find yourself getting angry with someone or something without knowing why?

- Do you ever find yourself having angry outbursts that are disproportionate to the event?

- Have you ever noticed that some people irritate you although you have little or no contact with them?

- Have you ever felt guilty, embarrassed or ashamed about certain behaviours and not known why?

- Do you ever put yourself down, judge or criticise yourself?
- Do you believe that on some level you are bad, evil or a mistake and should not have been born?

If you answered yes to any of the above questions (and most of us will probably have answered yes to all of them) your shadow is at work!

$$- \text{\textrulethunderbolt} -$$

Peter's story

Peter has spent some time in prison for attacking someone in a country pub. When a few of his old friends ask him where he has been for the past six months, he lies to them, telling them he has been working abroad. The reason for the lie is that he is so ashamed of his behaviour he cannot face the truth of his actions. He is afraid that people will withhold their approval or affection if he tells them the truth. He is terrified of the judgements and criticisms he will have to face. He believes he is a bad person because of his behaviour and that if he owns up to it, people will not want to be around him out of fear that he might turn violent again.

None of this, of course, is true. Peter has made it all up because of his own sense of shame and guilt. He finds it impossible to forgive himself and therefore can't believe anyone else will forgive him either. When old friends begin to probe him about his time spent abroad, he becomes defensive and touchy. They sense that something isn't quite right and drop the subject, but are left feeling suspicious of his behaviour.

How is the shadow formed?

The shadow is made up of those parts of our personality that we hide, neglect, disown, deny and repress (either consciously or unconsciously). We fear that if people were to find out that we think or feel these things, we might have to face painful chastisement, judgement or criticism from others. If these are people we value or hold in high regard, our fear of being found out in this way may be particularly acute. In order not to have to suffer terrible reprisals, we dissemble, concealing our reality and the truth. Thus the process of forming the shadow begins.

Consider the following:

If I tell my parents that I'm in serious debt again, I'm afraid they will disown me. I am deeply ashamed, so I lie to them about my financial status. I would be humiliated if they knew I had let them down and been a bad son. I am a bad person because I have disappointed my parents.

This shame is shadow material. And this is how it plays itself out:

When I meet others who are in debt or financial crisis, I silently criticise and judge them. I even find myself becoming openly hostile and aggressive, berating them for their irresponsible attitude. I become inflated and opinionated.

It is meeting others in the same situation that stimulates the shadow. These others reflect back at us our own guilt, shame and perceived shortcomings as human beings. Thus we feel threatened by them and do not want to be in their company – because it's too painful to look at our own shadow.

Repression

Events that have caused us a great deal of emotional pain in the past will be added to our psychic bag of shadow material. And if the event was particularly shameful or painful, our psyche will banish it to the nether regions of our unconscious, where we may completely 'forget' about it – or, in psychological terminology, repress it. But while repression may appear to have effected total memory loss, it often leaves a psychic trace in our reactions to an assortment of different situations. These reactions often have no apparent logical explanation and are out of our control.

Such reactions indicate that there is an underlying wound within us, and in order to heal this wound, we need to explore these reactions – preferably with the help of a therapist. Anything that is repressed controls us and will always return to haunt us – it's only a matter of time. Healing the wound means finding a way to come to terms with the dreadful memory we have repressed and so eliminating our inappropriate defensive thinking and responses towards others.

Everyone we meet potentially represents parts of us that we hide, neglect, disown, deny and repress. Everyone we meet is a potential teacher. The best teachers, of course, are the individuals we find ourselves reacting to most strongly. When this happens, we need to ask ourselves, 'What part of my shadow is this person mirroring for me now?' The more you ask yourself this question, the more of your shadows you will uncover, and the more shadows you uncover – and, more importantly, befriend – the freer you will be of reactive anger. (We will look further at ways of owning and befriending your shadows in Chapter Five.)

Clare's story

Clare is invited to the house-warming party of a close friend. When she arrives she walks into a room full of people. She notices a young woman across the room who is loud and boisterous and has gathered an enraptured crowd of men and women around her. To Clare it seems that they're all having lots of fun, but she feels excluded and too shy to go over and introduce herself.

Clare's feelings of exclusion make her increasingly irritated. She wants to be part of this gathering of happy, vibrant people but is not confident enough to join in. Instead, she stands alone, becoming more and more resentful of this woman and her audience. Clare begins to feel her anger rising against this woman. She fantasises about picking a fight with her, 'just to bring her down a notch or two'. She recognises that this anger is out of character for her and that it is beginning to overwhelm her. She is also starting to feel ashamed. She leaves the party without even saying goodbye to the friend who invited her, frightened by the anger and shame she has inside.

The following week in her therapy session, Clare shares her distress with her therapist and together they explore the triggers for Clare's anger and shame.

Clare discovers that beneath her chronic shyness is a fear of emotional contact that made her terrified to interact with the group of people having a good time.

The therapist suggests she consider that her fear was of being ridiculed or shamed by someone in the group, and that making herself vulnerable in this way was just too threatening for her. The only way she could deal with the situation was to project her insecurities onto the vivacious woman, who was in reality just having a good time with a few friends.

With the help of the therapist, Clare becomes aware of the part of her own shadow that she was projecting onto this woman. It becomes clear that for Clare being seductive, charming, girlish and sexually provocative is 'bad'.

The therapist asks Clare if she has ever expressed herself in these ways. Clare replies, 'If my mother ever saw me behaving like that she would kill me!' 'Kill you?' responds the therapist. 'Yes!' Clare says, then bursts into tears and shakes uncontrollably as she begins to understand that she has repressed her joy, her adventurous spirit, her sexuality and her dynamism in order to keep her mother happy.

Clare sees that in order to fit into her mother's model of reality she has had to split off many parts of herself. She recognises that she was jealous of the attention the other woman was getting. She wanted that kind of attention from other people too, but was too afraid to risk trying to get it in case it upset an internalised version of her mother, who was acting as judge and critic.

Now take some time out to think about what you have learned from this section and how you can start facing your own demons and healing yourself. Are you ready to start using some of the suggestions to help you manage your anger? There are plenty more to come, so and hang in there. You're doing great!

CHAPTER THREE

The Role of Anger in Our Lives

There is no old age for man's anger: only death.

—Sophocles

What would the world be like without anger? This was a question asked recently by a participant in one of my anger management courses. It was not one I had been asked before or had even thought about. I had always just taken for granted that anger exists and will always exist.

Anger has a function. Without it, we would probably live in a perpetual state of entropy. Anger is closely associated with will, and will is directly linked to our spirit. When we talk about someone being 'high-spirited' or having 'lots of spirit', we mean that they are alive, energised and motivated. They use healthy aggression to get things done. Anger drives us to make changes and accomplish things on the personal and global playing field. It motivates us to speak up and communicate our feelings, to define our boundaries and, above all, to protect ourselves from being taken advantage of. Healthy expression of anger gives us a voice. It says to the world: 'I am here. I exist. Take me seriously.'

The shadow side of anger is hell fire and brimstone. It is abuse of power, cruelty and destructiveness. In this chapter we will be looking at how, if we do not cultivate healthy ways of expressing it, anger can become a dark force, leading us to behave in self-destructive, manipulative and malicious ways on a personal, inter-personal and global level.

The goals of behaviour

Alfred Adler, a contemporary of Freud and Jung, developed a therapeutic model called individual psychology. He stated that 'we create conflict in order to get attention', even though the attention may be negative and can lead to further pain and misery. Creating conflict can also be a cry for help – although we may not necessarily know what help we need. Adler suggested that a person has four maladaptive goals of behaviour. Each goal reflects a lack of emotional awareness. In order for us to create emotional health, it is necessary for us to explore our negative behaviour and determine how it undermines us so that we can set about changing our destructive goals. When we understand the motivation behind the acting out of these goals, we can begin to make sense of why both children and adults sometimes behave in highly uncooperative and dysfunctional ways.

What's exciting about this particular model is that it enables us to see the way in which goals of behaviour emerged during our childhood and to identify the hidden agenda or subtext encoded in them. This agenda or subtext determines the way you live your adult life. With this knowledge, you can begin making the necessary changes to your behaviour – resulting in a reduction in stress levels, increased empowerment and an enhanced ability to control your anger appropriately.

The goals of behaviour are often concealed deep within the

shadow and so can be difficult to identify within ourselves. As such, they have become part of our deepest nature. They also have regressive components, which makes them harder to face up to and combat. Our task is to begin the process of understanding how they play out in our lives so that we can transcend our emotional limitations and manage our anger. We have to release ourselves from the past in order to get present – and remain present. With perseverance and the will to be truly honest, this can be accomplished. Facing up to our own maladaptive behaviour is a necessary part of becoming an adult in our own life. This is your responsibility and your challenge.

Let's now take a look at Adler's four maladaptive goals of behaviour.

1 Attention – by whatever means necessary

Attention from others gives us a profound sense of belonging. The need for such attention is part of the human condition, and most of us will do whatever we can to get it, even if that means receiving negative attention.

A child, for example, will complain, interrupt, whine and whinge until her parents pay attention to her, even if the attention comes in the form of her parents losing their patience and getting angry with her. Thereafter she may be quiet for a while, until she needs their attention again, when she may resort to a similar method of getting it – annoying or not! The only way the child can feel a sense of belonging is by being noticed by significant others, and preferably by everybody all of the time. Obviously, however, her strategy is not ultimately very effective, because she soon begins to irritate others and they start to take her needs less seriously. The more negative attention the child gets, the more desperate she becomes for positive strokes and encouragement. The more this need remains unfulfilled, the more obsessive she becomes about gaining attention – or she may completely withdraw into a state of deep depression. This behaviour is driven by her need for significant others to esteem her.

A child's need for attention is appropriate. When an adult wants this kind of constant attention, we often speak about them as being needy. When feeling insecure or bored, a needy adult does what he can to get attention from others – partly to distract himself from his painful inner feelings, partly to be reassured that he is OK, and partly to experience a sense of belonging and connectedness. If he gets attention, his self-esteem is increased, but not for long. The cycle of behaviour then begins again, and recurs, until such time as other people find it difficult to be around him.

A needy adult tends to frighten people away, which in turn makes him even more needy. It's a vicious circle. What this person actually needs is to identify his emotional needs and take responsibility for either meeting them himself or finding open, mature ways of getting them met by others. He needs to be explicit about what his needs are. If he can manage this, his attention-seeking behaviour will decrease and his self-esteem will increase, because he has learned to give himself attention and meet his own need for reassurance.

Attention-seeking is about continually testing others for love and devotion. Its subtext may be, 'As long as I keep their attention, they will never leave!' or 'The only way to have their attention is to keep them preoccupied with me.'

This kind of negative attention-seeking is particularly common among young people. Their disruptive behaviour is a demand for attention – a signal of distress and a call for help.

EXERCISE
DO YOU SEEK ATTENTION?

Take a moment to consider the following questions and answer them as honestly as you can, writing your responses in your journal.

- What do I do to get attention?

- What is the effect of my attention-seeking on others?

- What can I do to change my approach to getting attention?

— ⚡ —

2 Power struggles

Power struggles are about attempting to control others through manipulation and/or bullying. The basic dynamic at work – which is often unconscious – has to do with the desire for supremacy and control both in relationships and in situations.

Consider the power struggles that go on between parents and children. From an early age a child competes with his parents for power. Each tries to establish his or her superiority and show who is boss! For example, the child is asked to brush his teeth before going to bed. He resists and the parent insists. Now the issue is no longer about whether the child brushes his teeth or not; it is about who calls the shots around here! The parent's subtext is, 'Do as I say because I am in charge around here'; the child's subtext is 'No one bosses me around.' And, of course, the parent gets angry with the child, and the child gets very angry with the parent, and both may end up in tears.

This power struggle is exhausting for everyone concerned, but will continue until such time as the parent recognises that a power struggle is in fact being played out and makes a choice not to collude with her child's need for superiority and drama. Neither parent nor child can win in this situation, and both will go on feeling sad, angry and hurt until the struggle for supremacy is resolved.

As adults, we need to recognise the destructive and regressive nature of these power dynamics in our relationships – which means we have to learn that relationships are not about winning or losing but about sharing.

When I witness power games being played out amongst couples in my private practice, I challenge the competition between them. Often, they do not even recognise what has been going on. When the power struggle is obvious, I point it out to them and then give them an opportunity to see how being competitive serves neither of them. Usually they are then able to recognise this. I suggest to them that if they continue to compete, it's only a matter of time before the relationship fragments and they part company. In order to have a healthy relationship, cooperation, negotiation and fairness are vital.

The need to compete with others has its origin in the belief that the only way to belong and feel safe is to be in control. Relationships, however, are at their most creative when there is reciprocity. Relationships are about giving, taking and power-sharing. Win/win can be achieved through cooperation and negotiation – even if this takes months to achieve.

We will be talking about power in relationships in more depth in Chapter Four.

EXERCISE
HOW DO YOU USE OR ABUSE YOUR PERSONAL POWER?

Take a moment to think the following questions, then write your answers down in your journal. Consider your relationships with your family, your friends and your colleagues. This can be difficult stuff to face. Power – both having it and being at the mercy of someone else's – is scary. Be as honest as you can with yourself.

- How do I use my power in my relationships?

- How does my power serve me?

- How do I abuse my power in my relationships?

- What happens when others abuse their power in relationship to me?

— ⚡ —

3 Revenge

People who seek revenge usually feel unwanted, unloved and neglected. They are also inclined to create situations that will reinforce their sense of how unwanted and unlovable they are. Unconsciously, they believe that the only way they can belong is by hurting others in the way they have been hurt.

When we fantasise about hurting or taking revenge on others, we are in a state of emotional regression (we will be talking more about emotional regression in Chapter Five). And when we are regressed, we also try to regress those whom we feel have hurt us.

There are those of us who seem to love holding on to grudges and exacting revenge. In order to let go of this behaviour, we need to change our whole perception of ourselves and others – that is, we need to stop seeing ourselves as victims and, in some cases, accept that we are in fact ourselves responsible for perpetuating a lot of the problems we have in their lives. We also need to allow ourselves to experience our own sadness and grief. This may be what we resist most, fearing it will be too painful – but what we block out of our conscious mind is how painful our lives are already.

Asking a person to give up a grudge can be like asking a child to give up her security blanket. Who would they be if they had to do such a thing? Holding on to grudges and fantasising about revenge on some level serves to increase their inflated sense of potency. It also, however, keeps them isolated and angry with others. Those who have a chip on their shoulders or are spiteful and unnecessarily hostile towards others hold grudges as shields against further hurt and pain, and yet – through their actions and demeanour – they create conflict and hostility over and over again.

EXERCISE
DO YOU HOLD GRUDGES?

Think carefully about the following questions, then write your answers in your journal.

- Who am I holding a grudge against? (Make a list if this helps you gain more clarity.)
- How do these grudges serve me?
- What do I need to do in order to let go of these grudges?
- Who holds grudges against me, and why?

•

In Chapter Two we discussed shadow projections, the parts of ourselves we try to hide from ourselves and others, and that we react most strongly to in others. Revisit your notes on shadow projections in your journal and then answer these questions:

- Can you see any of your shadow projections being played out with the people you hold a grudge against?
- Can you see any of your shadow projections being played out with the people who appear to hold a grudge against you?

If you can, speak to these people and see if you can resolve any of these issues as a way of bringing closure to unfinished business from the past. You will find that you feel lighter immediately.

— ⚡ —

4 Learned helplessness

If a child is continually being told that she never does anything right or is never good enough, she will come to feel that she can have a sense of belonging only when others have no expectations of her. This engenders a profound sense of helplessness. When a child has not been encouraged or made to feel significant by her primary carers, she may give up on life, saying, for example, 'What is the point? I never get it right no matter how hard I try' or 'Everyone does it better than me.' Parents may treat a child this way out of their own negativity and general attitude towards life, without, perhaps, realising that children need encouragement and support to become cooperative and confident. It is important not to be critical of our children and to focus on their assets rather than fixating on their shortcomings.

As parents, we need to learn the difference between criticising the child's behaviour and criticising the child. When a child is criticised by a parent, she often feels deeply ashamed of herself. This shame instigates a learned helplessness cycle. This helplessness cycle seems an effective means of getting her needs met, although, in reality, she is not getting her needs met. In adulthood this behaviour translates into self-defensive anger and, of course, passive aggression towards oneself or hostility towards others.

EXERCISE

WHAT ARE YOUR EXPERI-ENCES WITH LEARNED HELPLESSNESS?

Consider the following questions carefully. Write your answers in your journal, together with any other thoughts that come into your head as you think about them.

- In what areas of my life do I feel helpless and a victim?
- In order to feel less helpless, what do I need to change, let go of or give up?
- When playing the role of the victim, can I recognise how I am giving my power away?

— ⚡ —

How we create conflict in our lives

We create conflict when we are in opposition to other people and have no awareness of the effects that our position exposes them to. One of the most effective ways to create conflict is to believe we are always right and that other people's opinions don't count. Many of us have grown up experiencing constant arguments and fights, and so we don't really know any different. Our spouse, however, might not have had the misfortune of growing up on a battlefield. The way we create conflict here is by assuming that our spouse – or friends or work colleagues – has had the same experiences as us and that conflict is a very normal experience.

EXERCISE

THE WAYS WE CREATE CONFLICT

Below are examples of how we trigger anger in each other. Read through them and see which ones you agree with; then reflect on why you feel the need to create conflict in your life in this way. What are you really trying to achieve? Be as honest with yourself as possible – you may be surprised by what you find out.

- **We don't listen to each other.**

  'I don't listen to you because I think you are less important than I am.'

  'I don't believe you are listening to me.'

  'I cannot concentrate for longer than a minute.'

- **We don't prioritise each other in our lives.**

  'You are not important to me.'

  'I am not important to me.'

  'I don't want to be responsible for your feelings and needs.'

- **We don't take each other's needs seriously.**

  'I am not serious about you.'

  'I don't take anything seriously.'

  'Why should I take things seriously.'

- **I don't take my own needs seriously.**

  'I don't take anything seriously, especially my needs.'

  'What needs?'

- **I don't have needs, do I?**

  'I make assumptions.'

  'I have spent my life making assumptions; why should I change now?'

'Usually my assumptions are correct, thank you very much!'

'I am a natural mind-reader.'

- **I don't do reality checks.**

    'Reality checks are a waste of time, I am never wrong!'

    'Why do we need reality?'

    'Everybody thinks the same things, don't they?'

- **We project our unmet needs onto each other.**

    'It's your fault that I am not happy.'

    'I know you're angry with me!'

    'I just hate it when he behaves like that towards me.'

- **I make 'you' statements rather than 'I' statements.**

    'You don't care for me.'

    'You always say things to hurt me.'

    'You never tell me you love me.'

- **I am not authentic in my own life.**

    'No worries, I am not hurt.'

    'Sure, I will get over it.'

    'I'm OK – but not really!'

- **I am not honest with myself or others.**

    'I really want to talk about it now.'

    'No, nothing's wrong.'

    'I am fine.'

- **I try to avoid conflict rather than dealing with it.**

    'I am really not angry with you.'

    'Just tell me you love me.'

    'We'll get over it.'

- **I want to be treated as special and different.**

    'You prefer her to me, don't you?'

'I can get away with it; he likes me.'

'I'm the boss here.'

• **I don't express your true feelings in the moment.**

'You are silent.'

'I am withdrawn.'

'You are moody.'

• **I take what others say personally.**

'Don't be so stupid.'

'Why don't you just grow up and act your age?'

'You will never learn, will you?'

• **I make comments about others without considering the impact they will have.**

'You really look terrible today.'

'I hate you!'

'It's your fault I have failed!'

— ⚡ —

What's at stake? – the consequences of our anger

Anger has consequences. If we are aggressive, we need to become aware of the effects of our outbursts. When we allow our anger to explode, however, we never consider what's at stake. Not only do we do and say things we will later regret but we also make ourselves a target for all sorts of abuse from others – and even run the risk of becoming a scapegoat.

Those of us whose anger style is implosive are all too well aware of the consequences of our actions – which is why we are imploders rather than exploders. However, we still have to deal with the consequences of our passive-aggressive behaviour – generally for ourselves – such as low-threshold depression. (For more about imploders and exploders, see Chapter Four.)

If you are prone to explosive anger, you need to remember this mantra: 'Back off, stop, think, take a look at the big picture'. Yes, of course it's hard, because when we feel threatened, our defence mechanisms kick in and our anger kicks out! But if we give in to explosive anger we are left with the negative fallout, which can include feelings of shame, remorse and depression.

If we can stop and consider the consequences of reacting with anger, we may find there is a way to resolve the conflict maturely without anyone having to experience the negative consequences of an explosion of aggression. This, of course, takes practice, practice and more practice.

EXERCISE
THE CONSEQUENCES OF ANGER

Completing this exercise will help you to step back and consider your strategy the next time you find yourself facing a challenging situation or person. It will enable you to avoid getting into a situation of open warfare with others.

•

Reflect on an argument you had recently. Consider the following:

• What were your needs?

• What were the other person's needs?

• Did you acknowledge your needs?

• Did you acknowledge their needs?

• What consequences did you experience from the conflict?

• What consequences did they experience from the conflict?

- How did you resolve the conflict?
- If you could go back in time, how would you deal with the conflict with the benefit of hindsight?
- If the other person could go back in time, how do you imagine they might deal with the conflict with the benefit of hindsight?

$$- \mskip1mu\text{\textasciitilde}\mskip1mu -$$

The four styles of conflict

There are four different styles of conflict. These are: healthy conflict, avoidant conflict, ambivalent conflict, avoidant/ ambivalent conflict.

Healthy conflict

Aim: To keep an open mind in order to create win/win situations

In this style of conflict, two people are able to argue while still remaining adult and responsible for their feelings. They are committed to some form of positive resolution, no matter what it takes to reach it. They work towards this respectfully, with an open heart and with mindfulness of how their behaviour may affect the other person. They are aware of what's at stake and are sensitive to the possible consequences. This type of conflict reinforces trust and deep intimacy.

Avoidant conflict

Aim: To avoid pain and shame at any cost

In this style of conflict we try to avoid conflict because it goes against our moral position and value system, and because arguing or getting angry engenders or reinforces feelings of shame in us. We dodge conflict in order to avoid pain and distress. The more we avoid conflict, however, the more our fear of pain increases. Eventually, nevertheless, the conflict comes to a head and erupts, leaving us to manage the fallout.

Fear of or resistance to conflict is particularly common among women, who may have been brought up to feel that anger is not feminine and is socially unacceptable in women. As a result they may go to great lengths to avoid it. But anger has a way of finding a release. It cannot – and should not – be avoided if we are to become fully rounded and whole human beings.

We all know that when it comes to dealing with conflict it's much healthier to resolve it in the first instance; otherwise it grows from a smoking ember into a forest fire – and then you're left dealing with scorched earth! If we leave things too late, the consequences can be extreme: our loved ones leave us, we get fired for misconduct, or we land ourselves in prison for grievous bodily harm because we attacked some unsuspecting stranger who was in the wrong place at the wrong time. By dealing with conflict promptly and effectively we can spare ourselves a lot of pent-up anger, worry and stress.

Ambivalent conflict

Aim: To choose not to choose

In this style of conflict we are overwhelmed by our own feelings and are therefore unsure how to proceed. We are in two minds about what to do or say. An example of this might be if you would like to tell your boss that you're angry with the way she is treating you, but you're afraid you might lose your job as a result, so you decide to say nothing. But anger doesn't just go away. It can reach the point where you feel so angry you cannot concentrate or do your job properly.

When you experience a conflict but are ambivalent about how to deal with it, it's better in the short term to contain yourself and seek support from your support network. Try to familiarise yourself with your own emotional discomfort until such time as the issue becomes less overwhelming for you. Then you can deal with it using the clearing process or the six key components of resolving disputes (see pages 199 and 213).

4. Avoidant/ambivalent conflict

Aim: To avoid pain and shame and to choose not to choose, hoping that somehow the decision will make itself

This style of conflict occurs where there are both positive and negative associations related to the decision-making process. It's the classic 'damned if you do, damned if you don't' scenario. Having to make a choice evokes 'avoidant–ambivalent conflict' in us – we cannot face making a decision, so we avoid the person or situation that causes us distress.

Evan's story

Evan so much wanted the approval of his boss that he found himself unable to confront him when he was consistently asked to work overtime without being paid. Evan's belief system was 'in order to excel in the world I need to be approved of by others'. Evan's wife was becoming increasingly irritated by his lack of courage and also began to take him to task. Evan was caught between a rock and a hard place because he also believed he needed his wife's approval in order to be loved by her. He slowly withdrew into himself and began to isolate himself. As he did this, he became more and more depressed. His work began to suffer, and eventually his boss confronted him about his sloppy work. Evan decided to hand in his resignation on the basis of too much stress in the workplace. He set about looking for another job and soon found one. After a couple of months in his new post, however, Evan found himself in a similar position with his new boss.

It is very possible that if Evan had confronted his first boss in a positive way, he would not have had to change jobs. He almost certainly would not have found himself in the same position again.

Anger and health

The pharmaceutical industry is enjoying record profits, and more and more people every year are turning to their GPs for treatment for psychologically aggravated illnesses. In a recent statistic, over 30 million prescriptions are given out annually for depression-related illnesses in the UK. Doctors have become alarmed by the high volume of drugs being prescribed for psychological illnesses. As an alternative they are suggesting that patients take more exercise as well as seek counselling.

It is becoming increasingly recognised that counsellors, psychotherapists, alternative and complementary therapists have enormously useful expertise to offer. Their services not only complement medication but also have positive long-term results and relieve the pressure on hard-pressed GPs. In Devon and Cornwall a group of people have even come up with the novel idea of getting doctors to refer patients to clinical librarians, who advise them on self-help and personal development books relevant to their psychological symptoms. There is much that we can do for ourselves to counter the rise of anger.

The role of stress

Anger and stress are two of the most significant contributors to ill-health and premature death in the Western world. The two are closely related, in that stress causes anger and anger causes stress. The more stressed you are, the more predisposed you are to becoming irritable and eventually angry. Being angry then stresses both you and those around you.

The people most at risk of stress are those who bottle their anger up and never get rid of it. The negative energy of their anger is trapped and held in the body. The body acts like a pressure-cooker; the anger builds and builds until, one day, the valve blows and the anger comes steaming out – more often than not, in the form of full-blown rage.

Stress can also be a health risk for those who are chronically angry or addicted to rage. Physical signs include a red face (indicative of high blood pressure), premature ageing, muscular tension and deep furrows on the forehead. The facial expression may be hostile and aggressive even when the person is not feeling angry.

Anger-related stress can be particularly detrimental to health where it translates into an addiction to drink or drugs. Such addictions arise as a result of the desire to escape repressed feelings, and can result in liver damage, brain damage and various forms of cancer.

Some of the other effects of anger and stress:

* High blood pressure
* Coronary heart disease
* Migraines and headaches
* Strained or red eyes
* Depression
* Insomnia
* Digestive disorders (irritable bowel, diarrhoea, ulcers, etc.)
* Deep muscular spasms in the back, shoulders and neck
* Skin disorders (eczema, dry skin, blistering, shingles)
* Loss of libido
* Cancer

Anger often takes up residence in a physical weak spot in the body. Being aware of where anger manifests in your own body can help you to become conscious of your emotional cycle and can help you to identify the early warning signs of an episode of anger. For example, if your back is a vulnerable area, you may experience twinges there when you start feeling annoyed. At this stage you can begin to use the rules of anger management to stop things getting out of control.

A result of practising anger management may be that we begin to feel physically better – and look better too. The symptoms of some of the health conditions above begin to diminish. This is because once we have begun to manage our anger in constructive ways, there is no longer a need to harbour unresolved strong feelings within the body, and our anger loses its toxicity.

Stress in modern life

'Stress is what happens when we try too hard and too often
to do the impossible'

C L Lake

The physiological stress response developed in primeval times as an aid to our survival in the face of danger. It involves the release of chemicals that enabled our distant ancestors to mobilise themselves to fight or run when they were in peril. Because their lives were highly physical, they were able to make good use of this mechanism.

Unfortunately for us, the challenges of modern life seldom involve the need for such a physical response, so we do not work off our stress in a healthy way. If you ran away from your workplace whenever things got on top of you, it would not win you any favours from your boss. And if you punched your boss on the nose whenever he gave you a tough time, the resulting dismissal and assault charges would generate considerably greater levels of stress. As a result, we simply accumulate adrenalin and other chemicals in our body.

The two forms of stress

Most of us see stress purely in negative terms – as a destructive, debilitating force. However, this is not entirely the case. A small amount of stress enables us to achieve a high performance and can be good for our health. You may be surprised to learn that we also experience a stress response as a result of positive experiences. The word 'eustress' has been coined to describe this phenomenon. Eustress results from exhilarating experiences. It is the kind of stress you are likely to experience if you inherit a large amount of money or receive an unexpected promotion. Eustress is the stress of winning and achieving.

Negative stress, on the other hand, is distress. It is related to losing, failing, overworking and not coping, and generally affects us in a harmful manner. We all experience this form of stress from time to time. It is a normal, unavoidable part of living. However, the almost constant state of stress in which many of us live, can compromise our mental and physical health.

The trick is to maintain a balance between positive and negative stress in our lives. We need to take control over the degree and frequency of the challenges we face so that stress works for rather than against us.

EXERCISE
WHAT'S YOUR TAKE ON STRESS?

Stress means different things to different people. To a mountaineer it might be reaching the limit of her physical resources as she attempts to scale a new peak. To a homeward-bound motorist it might be heavy traffic and noxious exhaust fumes. To a student it might be the pressure to pass an important exam. This exercise will help you to clarify what stress means to you.

- Write the word 'stress' at the top of a page in your journal.

- Sit quietly and think about this word, writing down all the words and images that come to your mind as you do so.

Managing stress

Stress used to be seen as an automatic response to stress-inducing factors in our lives or environment. Increasingly, however, it is being recognised that how we interpret or respond to potential stressors is in fact the crucial factor. That is, events themselves are not stressful; it is our way of responding that determines whether or not we will be stressed by them. This is good news, because it suggests that we can help ourselves by learning to deal with feelings and events in more creative and productive ways, thereby avoiding or reducing the impact of challenging situations.

Stress, then, results from failure to cope adequately with stressors. These stressors may be loud noises, uncomfortable air conditioning, debts, ringing telephones, broken relationships, unrealistic deadlines, discouragement, fear, pain or any one of the thousands of things that impact upon us in the normal course of life. It is impossible to avoid stressors. The only totally stress-free state is death! Stressors will always be there because we live in an imperfect and unpredictable world. Our body constantly seeks to maintain stability; when we experience stress the body has to make an adjustment that is just too challenging.

Scientists use the term 'homoeostasis' (*homoeo* = 'the same'; *stasis* = 'standing') to refer to the physiological limits within which the body functions efficiently and comfortably. Stress disturbs homoeostasis by creating a state of imbalance. The source of stress may be outside the body or it may originate from within the body in the form of high blood pressure, pain, tumours, disturbing thoughts and so on.

We need to develop special skills to deal with today's special stressors, both from a psychological and an emotional point of view. Exercise can be a great help in this respect, as it allows the body to release built-up tension and burn off adrenalin. Personal development skills that can help you to manage your emotional and psychological responses are also essential. We will be looking at stress management in more detail on page 102.

The effects of stress on the immune system

According to Dr Hans Selye, one of the pioneers of stress research, 'stress is essentially reflected by the rate of all the wear and tear caused by life'. As a result of his work in the field, he has become convinced that the body has only a finite reserve of adaptability to deal with the stressors of life. Selye likens this reserve to a bank account from which we can make withdrawals from time to time but into which we cannot make deposits. Another way to see this reserve is as a non-renewable source of energy, which will eventually be exhausted – with the result that we die. Some people squander their reserves and experience premature ageing as a result; others exercise more discretion and so maintain a reserve for longer.

Over a period of time the stress response begins to take a toll on the body. One of the prime sites affected is the thymus gland (a pale-grey gland that sits behind the breastbone, above the heart and that plays a key role in the immune system). The thymus pumps out millions of lymphocytes each day. Their role is to patrol the body killing off bacterial invaders. Specialised lymphocytes called macrophages literally eat invading bacteria. They operate in all parts of the body, and we depend on them for our survival. Macrophages are weakened by a steroid called cortisol that is released by the adrenal gland when we experience stress. This is why people under stress often experience more than the usual number of colds and illnesses.

Psychological stress does, then, have physical ramifications. Stressful thought patterns can do us a great deal of harm, flooding our body with stress hormones and undermining our immune system.

EXERCISE
REDUCE YOUR STRESS LEVEL

The questions in this exercise will help you to come up with steps to reduce the stress load you are carrying. Write your responses in your journal, together with any insights you gain.

•

Spend some time thinking about what stresses you out. Make a list of everthing you can think of. Leave nothing out. If possible, do this with one of your anger buddies or together with a group of other people. You will benefit from hearing other people's insights into their own stresses.

•

Spend some time exploring the effects that stress has had on your mind, body and spirit. Ask yourself how you feel about that. There is a cost incurred by stress. It is important to consider the price you are paying and whether you want to go on paying it.

•

Start to formulate an action plan to make healthy changes to your behaviour and attitudes that will mitigate the amount of stress in your life. Remember that small actions can have a significant effect and make your action plan manageable. Taking action is empowering; it will help to build your self-esteem and confidence.

•

Ask yourself what resistance you have to giving up stress. Consider what you need to let go of, change or give up. Are you willing to do this? This step is an important part of the process of stress reduction, because it is where we usually get stuck. In order to overcome our resistance, we need to look clearly at the effects of our current behaviours and what it costs us to keep them in place. Once we have identified these things, making changes generally becomes very easy.

•

Consider who you can go to to ask for support. Many of us have a lot of resistance to asking others for support or assistance, yet support is vital when it comes to managing our anger. Recognising that we need support reminds us that we are not alone and that we all need the encouragement of others in traversing some of life's more difficult terrains.

•

Think about rewards you can give yourself once you reach your goal. Kids love this part, so reward your inner child – make sure that once you have reached your goals, you give yourself a nice little treat or two! Rewards give you something to look forward to, while you are focusing your attention on making difficult changes to your behaviour and mindset.

— ⚡ —

Mike's story

As a result of completing the exercise above, Mike realised that he got very stressed out when driving his car through

London traffic – which he had to do frequently. The experience made him nervous, irritable and at times angry.

Having recognised the negative effects that city driving was having on him, he knew that he had to identify what other options were open to him. His first thought was public transport, but he hated public transport. Then he thought about using a bicycle; however, he had tried that before and found it too dangerous and too slow. Then he thought about a motorcycle. He says: 'That's what did it for me. Now I can get around London with no more stress and no more parking problems. I'm less agitated and irritable and that in itself is a huge reward.'

EXERCISE
STRESS   RECOVERY   CHART

Once you have completed the exercise above, you are ready to fill in a stress recovery chart like the one to the right. Read the examples I have given to see how the chart works, but use your own answers to the preceding exercise to complete your own chart. If you can, try to complete your action immediately so that your stress load is immediately reduced.

— *ϟ* —

Stressors	Effects – feelings	Action	Change	Support	Reward
1. Being in debt	Overwhelmed and scared	Devise monthly budget, set up savings account	Stop thinking I'm special and that I need to prove myself to others	Ask family and friends to check up on me weekly	A nice meal out once a month
2. Over-eating	Full, stuffed, lethargic scared, ashamed	Reduce intake of carbohydrates	Nourish myself from the inside	My wife, my coach and my friends	A new outfit once I have lost 5 kg
3. Being unfit	Stiff and de-energised, ashamed	Go to the gym and get a personal trainer	Recognise that I am not omnipotent	Ask my wife, my personal trainer and my friends for encouragement	A week's surfing holiday
4. Arriving late for appointments	Scared, ashamed	Pre-plan and improve time management	Being disorganised	My personal assistant	Spend an evening reading a good book
5. Getting into confrontations	Scared, confused	Use support to rehearse alternative ways of dealing with conflict	My need to be seen as perfect	My support network and my therapist	A trip to the theatre
6. Inefficiency	Resentful, angry	Communicate clearly regarding my needs and wants, hold people accountable	Learn how to be assertive, affirm to myself that I do deserve the best	Spend time with loving friends and positive, responsible people who make me feel good	Have a manicure
7. Pressure at work	Depressed	Be clear around boundaries, say no more often, thinking of the bigger picture	Make my health a priority over everything else	My husband and friends	Take up golf
8. Husband being absent a lot	Lonely, scared, anxious	Try new things, have more adventures	Have a more positive outlook and be more brave	Ask friends and family to encourage me and/or join in adventures with me	A weekend away on my own
9. Giving up my career	Loss of identity, sad, scared	Accept the loss and move on	Place importance on my own happiness rather than on having a career	Support from friends who understand that I am more than my career	Meal out with my husband
10. Cannot drive	Trapped, a feeling of failure, sad	Accept my limitations based on my choices	Stop beating myself up about not being able to drive	Ask friends and family to remind me that I have choices about what I can or cannot do	A day in a health spa

More suggestions for stress reduction

Try any of the following suggestions that appeal to you to reduce
your stress levels.

* Meditation
* Practise 'the power of now' – stay present in the moment
* Dance
* Martial arts
* Tai chi
* Yoga
* Exercise
* Non-competitive sports such as various types of fishing,
  sailing, rock climbing, etc.
* Relaxing hobbies such as painting, crafts, model building,
  etc.
* Gardening
* Listening to music
* Massage
* A sauna
* Relaxing with good friends over a meal
* Involving yourself in a pursuit that makes you feel
  passionate
* Cooking
* Walking the dog
* Ironing

Try anything that helps to calm your mind, release tension from your
body and keep you in the present, away from thoughts that create
anxiety.

Road rage

Road rage is the term coined by the media to describe an extreme reaction to a common modern stressor – the traffic on our increasingly busy roads. (Hot on its heels came air rage, trolley rage, tube rage, queue rage, mobile phone rage, computer rage ... and so on.) In many cases of road rage, however, what is being expressed is not in fact rage but anger. Rage is anger with its eyes closed (hence the expression 'blind rage'). It is anger totally out of control, and it can lead to violence or some form of desperate acting out. Generally speaking, individuals accused of road rage are venting their thoughts and feelings (albeit in an aggressive manner).

Where does road rage start? It may appear to begin with a specific incident on the road. However, this is not the real source. The seeds of road rage will have been planted hours, days, weeks or perhaps even years before. You may have had an argument with your friend, your boss or your partner. Then, while you are driving along, somebody makes an illegal turn or prevents you from entering a lane. It may be an action that threatens your safety or that of your family or others. It may be an action that leads you to feel diminished, disrespected, disregarded, or powerless. It may be only something that affects your expectations, for example that you will arrive on time. Whatever the situation, you've been reining your feelings in for so long that when a relatively ordinary annoyance or frustration comes your way, all of your anger finally comes steaming out.

The road rage scenario

In the heat of the moment, you lose your cool. Perhaps you are feeling upset and emotional. Anyway, you just react. You cut someone up in traffic or – worse – you engage in some form of verbal abuse or physical violence with another person.

Later, at the police station or across the solicitor's desk, you ask yourself, 'Why did I lose control? What's wrong with me?' And you start to realise that your anger may be a bigger problem than you thought.

EXERCISE
DO YOU HAVE A ROAD RAGE PROBLEM?

Ask yourself the following questions:

- Do I have a problem keeping my cool when driving?

- When I get angry in the driver's seat, do I feel that I am losing control?

- When I am angry, do I do things I later regret?

If your answer to these questions is yes, road rage is a problem for you. Remind yourself that:

- You will never resolve anger through physical violence.

- People who get violent are self-destructive.

- Using benign physical violence (for example punching a wall) to deal with your anger, is *not* a way of controlling your anger. Violence starts with walls. What comes next? Faces?

— ⚡ —

Avoiding road rage

If road rage is a problem for you, try the following tips for quelling it.

❋ Make sure the inside of your car is a pleasant environment – clean, comfortable, nice-smelling, with soothing music and, if possible, good company.

* Drive at a leisurely rate.
* Leave earlier than you need to or normally would.
* Map out the directions well in advance.
* Do your best to be empathetic with and polite towards other drivers.
* Leave law enforcement to the police.
* Courtesy is not a weakness; you can be flexible and still remain in control. For example, let other cars in ahead of you.
* Don't rise to the bait – refuse to react to aggressive or risky driving.
* Don't let the car change your identity – it's you not your car that has the power.
* Think in new ways that will help you to see the bigger picture (consider, for example that the other person may be lost and that's why he's driving strangely).
* Use supportive driving affirmations: 'I will have a safe, relaxed and enjoyable drive', 'I am happy to allow another car into my lane', 'Driving carefully gets me there safely.'
* Place stickers on your dashboard to remind you that road rage kills.
* Ignore other people's inconsiderate driving.
* Watch for aggressive or risky drivers and keep your distance.
* Pull over to the left lane and allow faster drivers to pass.
* Be prepared to admit to errors and apologise by using clear hand signals.
* Do not provoke other drivers by swearing, challenging eye contact or aggressive signals.
* Don't roll down your window and yell or threaten.
* Do not block the passing lane.
* Do not flash your high beams unnecessarily.

* Don't do anything that you wouldn't do face to face with another person.
* Don't take it upon yourself to punish another driver.

Your car is your own private domain, where you are in charge. Make it somewhere that feels safe and peaceful, not a war zone.

If I ruled the world ...

A colleague once told me that his daughter had been asked to write an essay entitled, 'If I ruled the world ...' I thought what an interesting assignment this would be for people with an anger management problem. In spite of what you may be thinking, in my experience most people who have difficulty managing their anger would dread and fear this level of responsibility, since they have little or no confidence in their own ability to enact control over any portion of their lives. For these people, an assignment such as this would pull into sharp focus some of their major issues around control.

Through exploring the subject of control with participants in my anger management groups, I have come to understand that almost every one of them believed that if they were not in control of their anger, then they were not in control of their lives or their world. And, as one of them put it, 'If I am not in control of my world, who is?' Group participants said they felt their anger was in control of their world. Most of them said they were not interested in having power or authority over other people; what they really wanted was enough self-esteem, independence, inner peace, financial ease and so on not to be controlled by others.

These people could all too easily recognise the huge responsibility that would be entailed by ruling the world, and it was not something they aspired to. To them, ruling the world equated with being responsible for the whole world. In our group work we explored how anger, because of its destructive nature, creates emotional instability, and can lead to an exaggerated or amplified need to be in control, yet the idea of being in control, even of their own world, seemed like a dream, a fantasy, not something achievable.

We went on to explore the effects that their negative behaviour had on the world – how it impacted on loved ones, how it made people scared of them, how it affected their physical and emotional health. In order to gain the 'right' amount of control in their world, we discovered that some key emotional resources were needed. These key resources are fundamental building-blocks for emotional literacy, and they increase meaning, safety and wellbeing in our lives. They are as follows:

* The ability to be honest with yourself at all times.
* The ability to be honest with others at all times, acknowledging that there may be times when honesty will affect someone else in a negative way.
* The ability to 'show up' in life. By this I mean having the integrity to take responsibility for your thoughts, feelings, behaviours, actions and values.
* The ability to be clear about saying yes and no, knowing that when you say yes you mean yes, and when you say no you mean no. This is an important aspect of creating healthy boundaries. Giving out mixed messages confuses not only others but also ourselves.
* The ability to be accountable. By this I mean that if you make a commitment to yourself or another, you follow through and fulfil your commitment. If you hold yourself accountable, other people trust you, and when other people trust you, your world immediately becomes a much safer place to be.

* The ability to communicate your feelings as and when you feel them. For example, when you feel happy, you say you feel happy; when you feel sad, you say you feel sad; even when you feel angry, you communicate this feeling in order for others to know moment by moment what you are feeling. I'm not suggesting that you take expressing your feelings to the extreme but that you begin the process of communicating your feelings in order to let others into your world.

* The ability to recognise when you are being hijacked by your own feelings, especially the feelings that get you into trouble – and you know which ones those are. It's important to recognise as you go into meltdown that you can take yourself outside the combat zone and activate all the information you have read and learnt. It does make a difference.

By being in control of your own life, you can experience the safety we all need. As you can now see, that this safety is based equally on developing healthy relationships in your life on a day-by-day basis. In the context of anger management, it is important to be aware that the more you allow yourself to feel, the more your anger will diminish.

So imagine ruling your world – it is possible, it is achievable. It does, of course, take time to arrive at this situation. Each of the bullet points outlined above takes practice on a daily basis. But gradually you will grow stronger, and ultimately you will be ruler of your own domain.

CHAPTER 4

Anger and Power

Power has many connotations, especially in abusive, angry settings. In its pure form, however, power is energy, and energy has consciousness. Power can be used to develop and nourish relationships, or it can be used to destroy them. Every time you use your anger inappropriately, you give your power away and abuse it. By exploring our relationship to power as a phenomenon, we can better support ourselves in managing our anger appropriately.

When I am talking about power relationships in my workshops I often notice that people's eyes begin to glaze over. We hear a lot about personal power and empowerment, and yet few of us are able really to relate these concepts to our everyday lives, or explore them in our personal relationships. We may associate power with those in authority, such as our parents, our teachers, gurus, the rich and famous, our boss, politicians and so on. The notion of having real personal power can be either scary or exhilarating, or both at the same time.

Becoming aware of power dynamics and how they get played out in our life, is a revelation and a turning-point for most of us, particularly with regard to understanding anger issues. It enables us to begin to make choices about how we deal with and manage situations where negative power dynamics are being played out.

The three types of power

There are three basic relationships to power. Two of them, power-lessness and seeking power over, are unhealthy; the third, empowerment is healthy.

Powerlessness

Those who fear their own power tend to disempower themselves in subversive and sophisticated ways. They may blame others for the things that go wrong in their lives, perhaps feeling hard done by them. On the other hand, they may blame themselves for being so incompetent, feeling that whatever they do is not good enough.

Seeking power over

Despite what I have said above, there are a small number of people who become excited or exhilarated by the idea of having power over others (as opposed to having their own intrinsic sense of power). These people tend to be abusive, controlling or disrespectful towards other people. This behaviour is usually a compensation for deeper feelings of inadequacy.

Empowerment

Empowerment is a healthy sense of power that arises from within. It does not depend upon having someone to dominate. Those who feel empowered are supportive, encouraging and empowering of others. They listen to and see others without making value judgements.

Having power/lacking power

Our personal power is contaminated by our inability to acknowledge and accept ourselves, others and situations as they are, in the moment. We abuse our power because we lack emotional awareness of ourselves or those around us. Of course, eventually we have to take responsibility for our actions, thoughts and feelings. We could lose our job, our friends, our family, our income, our self-esteem, our dignity and our health. In extreme cases, we may even end up serving a jail sentence for injuring someone very badly. If we refuse to cultivate awareness of how our behaviour affects others, we will eventually be made aware of this when someone tells us what we don't want to hear, forcing us to distinguish, discern and differentiate between appropriate and inappropriate behaviour. And if this doesn't happen, we will start to notice that people stay away from us because of our inconsistent, disrespectful and abusive behaviour.

Most of us misunderstand power dynamics, and this inevitably influences the way we think and feel about ourselves and others. This misunderstanding influences our families, the education system and the workplace.

For many of us, our early experience to power was as something wielded by our parents like a dangerous sword, to make us perform and obey while living under their rule. Their motivation was partly to socialise us and partly to make their lives less chaotic so that the home could be run without too many disruptions or crises. The result is that from a very early age, even before we were aware of ourselves in relationship to others, most of us were being controlled, manipulated and offered conditional love. 'Yes, you can have a biscuit if you behave yourself,' or 'If you're a good little girl, I'll buy you that lovely dress we saw the other day.' From this kind of conditioning we learn that 'good' and 'bad' behaviour are what our carers want and don't want us to do. However, as we grow up, we also have to assimilate many different value systems – that of school, that of our friends and eventually that of the workplace – each with their own set of beliefs about what is appropriate behaviour. Given the many mixed messages we receive as we grow up, it's inevitable that our relationship to power and control can become dysfunctional.

The two power dynamics we are discussing here, having power

and lacking power, are symptomatic of something called closed system thinking – that is, the (mistaken) belief that there is not enough power to go around. If we believe there is not enough of something to go around, we become over-protective of our possessions, whether these are material or exist in the realm of the pysche or the emotions. Thus if our belief system is oriented towards a lack of abundance, we will be hyper-sensitive about everything we own.

This attitude, of course, spills over into our relationships. Our belief system reinforces that in order to feel powerful, we must have ownership. Therefore if we believe that someone is threatening our possessions, we become angry and fight by any means to reclaim what is ours – be it by domination, control or manipulation. This scenario is also played out whenever we believe we have a claim of ownership over a person, for example our spouse, our partner, our children, our friends, our employees and so on.

Jealousy is a symptom of the belief that power equates with ownership. Jealousy is a consequence of low self-esteem and a deep insecurity based on the negative self-belief that we are not good enough and that other people pose a threat to our exclusive right to the love and attention of those we are attached to. If from an early age we have internalised the belief that there is not enough of anything to go around, we watch out jealously for any potential threat to people, things, thoughts, ideas and dreams. Whenever we feel threatened, we believe that these things will be taken away from us – and that if they are, we will lose our power. Sadly, we often create a self-fulfilling prophecy, for the more tightly we to cling to the people in our lives, the more likely we are to drive them away.

EXERCISE
HAVING POWER/LACKING POWER

This exercise will help you to discover how the having power/lacking power dynamic manifests in your own life. Ask yourself the following questions, writing down the answers in your journal:

- In which areas do I feel the most powerful in my life?
- When am I the least powerful in my life?
- In which areas do I feel the most powerless in my life?
- When do I feel the most powerless in my life?
- How do I use my personal power?
- How do I abuse my personal power?

If you answer these questions fully, you will find that there is much information to be gleaned about yourself from this process. This will help to support you in managing your anger and in becoming more assertive in areas where you currently allow yourself to be manipulated by others.

— ⚡ —

Sharing power

Many participants in my anger management workshops tell me that the reason they are there is because their anger has turned to violence. When they find themselves being violent they get scared, because their inability to stop their violent outbursts reinforces their belief that they have absolutely no control over their feelings and impulses.

How we use (or misuse) our power is based, in part, on the meaningfulness of particular relationships to us. A meaningful relationship is one in which we can communicate freely and honestly. We feel that all of who we are is accepted, acknowledged and loved unconditionally, with the result that we can express all the parts of ourselves, the light and the dark. If a relationship is meaningful to us and we can communicate well in it, we feel less anxious and threatened because we are secure in the knowledge that we can be open, speak our mind and express our feelings. This supports our own personal growth and development. In meaningful relationships, we share the power rather than fight to monopolise it.

When a relationship is not meaningful to us, on the other hand, we may use our power to control and manipulate it. We believe that we have less to lose, so we act as we please. We are less emotionally invested in what the other person thinks of us, so being abusive or insensitive is irrelevant to us. We may become aggressive and hostile, often without even being aware of it. This behaviour is, of course, unhealthy, and certainly does not encourage further intimacy. Everyone deserves respect. If we look honestly into our soul we can recognise that when we are hostile and abusive it is because we feel threatened in some way.

Even in relationships where power-sharing is the norm, however, problems can arise when a threat is perceived from someone or something else. We may find our anger barometer beginning to rise and our internal defence systems activated. All of a sudden, we have turned into a war machine, prepared to do combat at any cost.

We can all use our power to keep ourselves safe and out of trouble or to cause a good deal of it. Whether we do the former or the latter depends on our level of self-awareness.

EXERCISE
POWER GAMES IN YOUR RELATIONSHIPS

In every relationship we have there is always some degree of power struggle taking place. In some relationships this struggle will be benign and in others it will be aggressive and full of power play. This exercise is designed to enable you to identify benign power relationships in your life.

•

Make a list of ten people with whom you get on very well.

•

Look at each person on your list in turn and see if you can identify what it is about them that helps or enables you to get on so well with them. After each person's name write: 'I get on well with — because ...'

•

When you have considered each person on your list, see if there are any common features among your reasons for getting on with them.

•

You will probably discover that one thing all these people have in common is that they do not threaten you. You feel safe with them. Why is this? Because there are no power games being played between you. When you are together, you exercise your power in an open healthy way, without trying to dominate or manipulate one another.

— ⚡ —

Letting go of the need for power over

As a result of reading the above sections, you should now be a little clearer about how power gets played out in your life. You may have come to see that in order to feel safe in the world, you believe that you need to be in control of all situations and personal relationships at all times. This is, of course, not true; it's just that your personal belief system tells you this is so. Once you start sharing your feelings with others and talking about your anxieties, fears and shame, you can begin to dismantle this misunderstanding. As we become increasingly empowered from the inside, our need to control others eventually becomes obsolete – it's only a matter of time!

Take a moment now to think about key learnings from this chapter so far. Don't worry if things are still not completely clear in your mind. Just keep turning them over in your thoughts about the different aspects of power and how they affect your life.

The five anger styles

When you are angry with someone, what approach do you use to express your anger? In his book *Facing the Fire*, John Lee suggests that there are four anger styles: intimidator, interrogator, poor me and distancer. I would like to add another that I recently discovered with the help of some participants on one of my weekend workshops, the winder-upper. Let's now take a look at each of these styles.

1 The intimidator

* Our intention: to control others by using an aggressive stance.
* Our belief: 'If the person is scared of me, they will do exactly what I want them to do.'
* Our behaviour: giving the evil eye; eye-balling; finger-pointing; an aggressive stance; shouting; body posturing;

> making threatening, intimidating and patronising
> statements and gestures.

With this style of anger, we seek to control others in a very aggressive way. We steal energy by harassing others into paying attention to us so that we can get what we need from them. We believe this is the only way we can get our needs met. Anger management programmes are full of intimidators.

Have you ever seen yourself as a bully, or even a petty tyrant? Has anyone ever suggested that your behaviour can be abusive and threatening? Have you ever found yourself screaming and shouting, hurling abuse at others, making threatening statements, or pointing a finger or eye-balling other people when you find yourself not getting your own way? This is classic intimidator behaviour. I'm aware, for example, that I myself am inclined to intimidate others when I feel out of control and scared and am too afraid to communicate this. I conceal to myself what I am feeling and try to manipulate my environment to get my needs met by intimidating everyone around me in order to regain control.

Being an intimidator is about invoking fear in others in order to control them, and fear is a highly effective tool. It is important to remember that when you intimidate someone else, you are scaring them in order to get them to do something for you that they have resistance to doing.

There can be a fine line between aggression and assertiveness. However, whereas assertiveness can lead to clarity, aggression leads to abuse! Assertiveness is about knowing what you want and getting it respectfully, without maliciously hurting those around you. The difference is in the intent. If the intent is to manipulate, control and have power over others, this is aggression.

The world sometimes expects us to be an intimidator, especially if we're a man. Aggression is often admired and expected, for example, in the workplace and on the sports field. Unfortunately, many men think it's cool to be aggressive, and may lose the ability to behave in any other way, feeling awkward in environments where gentleness, tenderness and respect are necessary. Such men lack the ability to consider the feelings of another, to empathise and to have compassion – either for themselves or for other people – and this leaves them increasingly isolated. Hurt and unhappiness are reinforced when we are unable to adjust and adapt to situations where aggression is not tolerated.

All behaviour is learned, however. Those of us who are character-istically aggressive can learn to become assertive by recognising the impact that our behaviour has on others and making a commitment to doing something about it. Intimidation serves no one. It's far healthier to communicate how you feel, for example by saying, 'I feel angry with you, and when I feel angry all I want to do is hurt you.' Begin the process of sharing how you feel moment by moment. It will take courage to start with, but it will become easier. The following exercise will give you insight into the origins of your intimi-dating behaviour.

EXERCISE
INTIMIDATION

Ask yourself the following questions. Write your answers in your journal.

- Who did you learn your intimidating behaviour from?
- Who has intimidated you?
- How did it feel?
- Did you feel manipulated?
- Did you feel angry?
- What did you do with your anger?

2 The interrogator

With this style of anger, we seek to control others in a more manipulative way, using questions to find fault and make others feel self-conscious, guilty, embarrassed, ashamed and monitored.

* Our intention: to get others to see things our way. We use a machine-gun spray of questions intended to make others experience their behaviour as inappropriate, bad or shameful.
* Our belief: 'I have power and control over how you feel and think; you will feel bad and obey me without question.'
* Our behaviour: asking lots of questions such as: 'What time do you call this?', 'Who do you think you are?', 'Where do you think you're going?', etc.

You may have been on the receiving end of the interrogator if, as a teenager, you ever came home in the early hours all bleary-eyed and much the worse for wear. You may recall a barrage of questions from one or both of your parents – questions intended to make you feel guilty and ashamed. For example, your mother may have looked at her watch and asked, 'What time do you call this?' – already knowing the time full well – the subtext to this early morning rhetoric being, 'I am furious with you and am going to make you feel as guilty as hell'. This is the style of the interrogator. Do you recognise it within yourself? If you have children of your own, you probably do.

Many parents use this style to invoke guilt and shame in their children, believing that it is an effective tool in controlling their behaviour. This style is the one most used by people who feel they have power over others. If you recognise this behaviour in yourself, you need to learn to share openly with others the fact that you feel angry with them, why you feel angry and the effect that their behaviour has on you. You might say, for example:

*I'm feeling angry with you because you said you would
be back at 10 and it's now 12. I feel disrespected and I was
getting frightened that something had happened to you.
Please do your best to be home on time in future, and if
you know you're going to be late, ring me – even if you're
afraid I may be angry. Is this understood?*

EXERCISE
INTERROGATION

Ask yourself the following questions. Write your answers
in your journal.

- Who did you learn your interrogatory behaviour from?

- Who has interrogated you?

- How did it feel?

- Did you feel manipulated?

- Did you feel angry in response?

- What did you do with your anger?

— ⚡ —

3 The poor me

With this style of anger, we seek to control others by making them
feel guilty for not doing enough for us. We are able to steal energy
from them when they buy into this guilt trip. When they give us the
attention we are looking for, we believe that we have gained power
over them through our manipulating and controlling tactics.

- ✹ Our intention: to gain attention from others by making
  them feel ashamed because they have neglected and
  mistreated us in some way.

* Our belief: 'The only way I can have power in the relationship is by making you feel guilty about the way you have treated and behaved towards me.'
* Our behaviour: we say things like 'I try so hard to help you and all I get is a mouthful of abuse', 'No one really understands me', 'I slave over a hot stove for you and you can't even get home on time', 'You're so selfish; you never think of what I want!', 'Why am I such a failure?' (Note: whining and moaning are anger through a small hole!)

I learned from a very young age how to manipulate others through learned helplessness (see page 87). This behaviour is very effective and to some extent appropriate when we are young. The problem is that if we do not grow out of learned helplessness as we grow up, in adulthood it becomes very difficult to give up. In learned helplessness, our actions cry out for someone to rescue us, take care of us and protect us. The result, however, is that we remain imprisoned by our fear of taking responsibility for our own lives. The 'poor me' who suffers from learned helplessness needs to find the courage to recognise how this behaviour is sabotaging their lives and undermining potentially healthy relationships with others.

While the 'poor me' is a manipulator, they also sometimes end up being manipulated by others. If this happens, they will express their resentment – occasionally to the point of verbally or physically abusing others, although this sort of behaviour is uncharacteristic. While primarily an imploder, the 'poor me' will eventually explode. Unfortunately, the result is often that they feel so much guilt and shame about exploding that they never let it happen again – although, of course, unless they take steps to understand and change their behaviour, it's only a matter of time before it does. (For more about imploders and exploders, see page 132.) If they go on swallowing their anger, the 'poor me' can end up depressed – even clinically depressed in severe cases.

If you recognise the 'poor me' in yourself, you need to learn how to become assertive in your life, to identify what you need and then make sure you get it in straightforward, mature ways. This requires courage and honesty with yourself and others, but it can be done. The following exercise will help to set you on the right path.

EXERCISE
POOR ME

Ask yourself the following questions. Write your answers in your journal.

- Who did you learn 'poor me' behaviour from?
- Who has used 'poor me' behaviour towards you?
- How did it make you feel?
- Did you feel manipulated?
- Did you feel angry in response?
- What did you do with your anger?

— ⚡ —

4 The distancer

With this style of anger, we seek to control others by remaining detached, aloof, secretive, withholding and vague.

- ❋ Our intention: seducing someone into chasing us around in order to probe and figure us out so that we can gain energy from their attention.
- ❋ Our belief: 'The other person will guess I am angry or upset and will follow me to acknowledge and respond to my anger.' The distancer may also believe that if they do not

deal with their feelings of anger, these feelings will subside and disappear.

* Our behaviour: the classic quality of the distancer is to do everything possible to avoid conflict, intellectualising every feeling. The distancer describes feelings as if they were thoughts: 'I don't have a problem with anger, never had, never will', 'I never get angry', 'I'd rather run away than get angry', 'The only time I ever get angry is when you make me angry', 'I have not been angry in years'.

The distancer will give you the silent treatment and diminish their feelings, because allowing themselves to feel threatens their sense of self.

I find that when distancers attend one of my anger management programme, they seldom come of their own accord. They will say they are there because they have been sent by their spouse or by their company. Often, they will claim to be there out of curiosity, believing that they do not have an anger issue, even though their family, friends and colleagues, repeatedly tell them differently. After a few hours they usually concede that they do have an anger management problem, but it sure takes energy to convince them of it.

I often get asked whether walking away from conflict is a way of distancing. Firstly, it is very important to recognise that walking away does not mean that we are running away or that we are weak. Walking away gives us time to stop, reflect and take a look at the bigger picture. Then we can return to the conflict and talk clearly and openly about our thoughts and feeling. Distancers, on the other hand, walk away and on their return (if they do return) do not deal with the issues raised in conflict. They often feel a deep fear of attempting to resolve the conflict in case it turns into a forest fire.

If you are a distancer, you need to learn how to open up and share your feelings with others without being afraid of things going wrong

wrong. Familiarising yourself with the territory of emotional pain will enable you to communicate without anyone getting hurt, and, furthermore, it will create intimacy and deepen links with loved ones. Expressing makes for much healthier relationships than running – and eventually you will run out of road and will have to work on your personal development if you want to remain healthy.

EXERCISE
DISTANCING

Ask yourself the following questions. Write your answers in your journal.

- Who did you learn distancing behaviour from?
- Who has used distancing behaviour towards you?
- How did it make you feel?
- Did you feel manipulated?
- Did you feel angry in response?
- What did you do with your anger?

— ϟ —

5 The winder-upper

With this style of anger, we seek to control others by joking, making fun of, mocking and teasing others. Our anger is expressed as a joke, but there's always a barb attached to it. Winder-uppers use their anger not just to define themselves and test people's love but also to get other people to express their unexpressed anger. In this way they can express their anger through the back door and don't need to take responsibility for their own feelings.

The irony is that this type of person is someone few people are prepared to tolerate, and a disagreement will often turn into fireworks. People tend to avoid the winder-upper at all costs, which leaves them isolated and potentially even more angry, hence reinforcing their negative core belief about not being lovable.

* Our intention: to get others to express our unexpressed feelings and emotions, especially our anger.
* Our belief: 'By putting others down I feel better about myself. If I can get others to feel and express my unexpressed anger, then I don't have to deal with my own distressing feelings.'
* Our behaviour: saying something derogatory or patronising and then, when others react to them, responding by saying, 'Can't you take a joke?', 'You're always so serious; chill out', 'Lighten up a bit, mate; no need to get so uptight with me', 'You sure are menstrual this month'.

As I mentioned earlier, this style of anger was defined recently by a participant in one of my anger management programmes. The reason I had not recognised it before myself is because it was part of my shadow. I spent most of my childhood and adult years, winding people up, irritating them and generally pissing them off in order to get them to express my anger for me. Of course, I was doing all of this unconsciously.

The sad thing about the winder-upper is that he quickly alienates everyone, yet without being conscious of the effect his behaviour has on others. He is usually oblivious to other people's feelings and has absolutely no understanding of the impact of his words. He is also very good at giving mixed messages. He likes to make fun of someone and then, just as the other person is becoming angry, quickly change tack and say something like, 'A little touchy today, aren't you?'

The winder-upper alternates between imploding and exploding, and all his jokes are passive-aggressive in nature. He also tends to avoid people who are assertive enough to tell him that his jokes are not funny and that he should immediately back off. Nevertheless, he always manages to have a few victims hovering around at any given time. Making other people the butt of his humour is, of course, a way of getting attention and of showing everyone how 'clever' he is.

EXERCISE
WINDING PEOPLE UP

Ask yourself the following questions. Write your answers in your journal.

- Who did you learn winding-up behaviour from?
- Who has used winding-up behaviour towards you?
- How did it make you feel?
- Did you feel manipulated?
- Did you feel angry in response?
- What did you do with your anger?

— ϟ —

Each anger style has its own unique destructive flavour and distinctive quality. We can use each style separately or we can use them in combinations depending on the result we want to achieve. Sometimes we are not even sure of the result we want to achieve, but nevertheless we thrash around blindly until we create some effect. Only then do we come to our senses, if we are lucky, and become aware of our intention, which is usually to hurt another person emotionally or to gain power and control over a situation or person.

Within the space of a minute we can use many different combinations of anger styles. If a particular style is not having the desired effect, we may add another one – and another – until we get the result we want. This usually goes on completely unconsciously, without us even noticing when we shift from one anger style to another. I have personally noticed myself using all five styles within seconds of each other!

Controlling our anger takes discipline, awareness and a firm intention to stop our abusive behaviour. The following exercise will help you to become more aware of when you use the various anger styles.

EXERCISE
WHEN DO YOU USE THE DIFFERENT ANGER STYLES

Look at each anger style and consider the situations in which you use it. I have given you a few examples to get you going.

- **I use the intimidator when:**

    I want to get a quick reaction from others.

    I know that I can manipulate you into doing what I say.

- **I use the interrogator when:**

    I want to shame someone.

    I feel insecure and want to be in control.

- **I use the distancer when:**

    I want you to make things better for me.

    I am afraid of hurting your feelings.

- **I use poor me when:**

    I want you to feel sorry for me.

    I want you to take care of me.

- **I use the winder-upper when:**

  I am afraid to confront you directly.

  I feel like you have hurt me.

— ⚡ —

Exploders and imploders

As we have seen, anger takes a wide range of forms. There is rage, hostility, aggression, fury, resentment, assertiveness and so on. Each of these behaviours can be either low or high in explosivity.

Most of us associate displays of anger with 'exploders' – that is, those of us who aren't shy to raise our voices and demonstrate our discomfort and dislikes in loud and abusive tones. However, there is another cluster of people who remain within a subterranean zone where anger manifests itself as a dark, brooding force. In this instance, anger is expressed sideways, in sarcastic comments, in moods or silences, perhaps even in devious plotting – though without confronting the other person involved. This is passive-aggressive behaviour, the behaviour of the imploder.

Exploders

Exploders can move from anger to full-on rage in an instant. Their anger is irrational. Once they begin to act out aggressively, they are in a state of emotional regression and become dangerous to themselves and others. Not long after their temper-tantrum they regret their outburst and their dysfunctional behaviour – but by then, of course, it's too late and the damage is done.

Exploders are unable to look at the big picture. Their rational brain has been hijacked by the older instinctive brain and adrenalin coursing their bodies (see page 46), and there's no telling what they may do. When alcohol also enters the scene, the exploder is at his or her most dangerous and violent.

Exploders know intrinsically that it's only a matter of time before their whole world crumbles and they end up alone, scared and depressed because of all the chaos and destruction they have caused themselves and others.

Exploders need to learn:

* To contain these overwhelming primitive feelings
* To look at the bigger picture
* Not to take things personally
* To delay gratification
* To sit in the discomfort of their own powerlessness, helplessness, fear, shame, hurt and anger
* To make anger their ally
* To stop seeing others as the enemy
* To develop a healthy relationship with their shame and the contents of their shadow
* To relax and meditate
* To find healthy outlets for their aggression

In Chapter Seven, we will be looking at the eight golden rules of anger management – the key tools for controlling and containing explosive anger.

Think about the preceding section. Ask yourself, 'Do I
recognise myself as an exploder?' If so, make a list of your
exploder behaviours in your journal.

$$- \text{\textit{ϟ}} -$$

Imploders

Imploders swallow their anger. They bottle it up for long periods of
time, for reasons of fear, insecurity and low self-esteem. Imploders
are terrified of both their own and other people's anger and fear
rejection and abandonment. Once they recognise that they can be
rejected and abandoned only by themselves, they become
courageous and heroic.

This process is beautifully illustrated in the film *Anger
Management*, in which Adam Sandler, who is an imploder, begins to
take back the personal power he formerly gave to others in order to
be liked. As he becomes increasingly empowered, his low self-
esteem, fears, anxieties and insecurities dissolve, to the point where
he finds himself becoming increasingly aggressive as he accesses his
new-found strength. He turns into an exploder and becomes violent
towards his original foes. Eventually, in some of his relationships,
he starts to learn how to be assertive rather than agressive.

Imploders do not always turn into exploders on the road towards
healthy expression of anger; however, some do – often those people
who have spent most of their lives being bullied. Once they find their
courage, it's pay-back time, and they make others suffer at their
hands. (In other cases where people have suffered from bullying, they
vow as a result never to hurt anyone; they are empathetic to the suffering of others around them and are receptive to the needs of others.)

As you know, I spent most of my life as an imploder (see page 2) – and when I stopped imploding, all hell broke loose! It was as if all the years of implosion could no longer be contained. I was just spilling out of myself. Through this experience, I learned the two most important lessons of my life. They were:

* It's none of my business what other people think of me, and I don't need to turn this into a drama.
* If you don't like me that doesn't mean I am unlikable.

These two statements became my mantras for years, and initially they helped to transform me. From imploding I moved to dispersing all my energy through exploding, and from there I finally moved to assertiveness. I became firm about saying yes and no, and I stuck to my guns.

Turning our anger in on ourselves may appear on the surface to cause us little harm, but we cannot go on doing this forever; we have to let it out. An imploder is a walking time-bomb. The longer their anger is held in, the more damage it does them, both physically and emotionally. As irrational as the exploder may seem, the imploder is in fact more so. Imploders stack dominoes of emotion and pain – and we all know that when the first domino is knocked over, all the others fall down. And all it takes to knock over an imploder's first domino is a seemingly insignificant event occurring at the wrong time.

Imploders need to learn:

* To deal with their fear of being abandoned and rejected
* Not take things so personally
* That they have a right to express and communicate their feelings and needs
* That they have a right to exist!
* To stand up for themselves

* To be clear about their 'yes' and their 'no'
* To hold their ground and not budge once their decision is made
* Not just to agree in order to avoid conflict
* To be less nice and more honest with themselves and others
* To acknowledge that they also have needs
* To recognize that they are a priority in their own life
* To befriend their anger
* To develop a healthy relationship with their shame and the contents of their shadow
* To relax, meditate and find ways of de-stressing

EXERCISE
ARE YOU AN IMPLODER?

Think about the preceding section. Ask yourself, 'Do I recognise myself as an imploder?' If so, make a list of your imploder behaviours in your journal.

— ⚡ —

Clean and unclean anger

In this section we're going to be looking at how we can use and express our anger healthily and assertively (clean anger) without imploding or exploding (unclean anger) through what we have come to call 'clean' and 'unclean' anger.

As the name suggests, there's nothing messy about clean anger. It is anger communicated assertively, without high drama, threats, challenges and abuse attached to it. It simply says to the other person, 'I am angry with you and what I need is …' (In Chapter Six we will be looking at a simple clearing process that you can use to express your anger without anyone getting or feeling hurt.)

The following is a simple way of understanding clean anger:

C cooperative
L learning/listening
E empathetic
A acknowledging
N nourishing/nurturing
A asserting yourself
N non-violent
G goal-orientated
E ethical
R responsible

Unclean anger is used with the intention of hurting or abusing someone because we feel they have hurt us in some way.

The following is a simple way of understanding unclean anger:

U unkind
N needy
C cruel
L lazy
E exaggerated
A arrogant
N neurotic
A aggressive
N non-negotiating
G greedy
E empty
R raging

Unclean Anger

Unclean anger springs from our deepest recesses and is linked to our primal instincts. It is experienced as an automatic way of thinking which can reflect distorted patterns. If we really examined some of our statements we would see the distorted structure of our thinking patterns, and upon further investigation we would see how they are directly linked to our defense mechanisms. Such thinking is not always unreasonable – indeed, it can lead to quite appropriate responses – but at other times it may be linked to repressed childhood memories. Unclean anger is an automatic response.

From the following examples below see if you can recoginsie some of your own distorted thinking.

Trivialising

Trivialising is treating something as – or trying to make it appear – less important, less significant or less valuable than it really is.

When we trivialise another person or their experiences, we bring our defence mechanisms into play, perhaps by trying to discount the other person's experiences or to demean them, and this passive-aggressive strategy may be highly effective. We may behave in this way because we have been hurt – perhaps because we feel that the other person is trivialising our own experiences (which may or may not be the case).

Examples of trivialising language are:

* You've got to be joking!
* Anyone can do that; it's so easy!
* Why are you acting so stupid?
* It's only a cat; we can get another one.
* Stop being so emotional.
* You can do much better than that if you try.
* You wish you had the brains!

* How come you can't do it? Everyone else manages.
* Your mum cooks much better than that.

EXERCISE
HOW DO YOU TRIVIALISE?

Make a list of words or expressions that you find yourself using when you are trivialising.

* How many of these expressions have been used against you?

* Consider how you could change your language in order to reduce the anger and animosity that are concealed within trivialising anger. For example:

  * Anyone can do that; it's so easy! / If you put your mind to it you can do it!

  * Why are you acting so stupid? / This seems difficult for you. Is it?

  * It's only a cat; we can get another one / You look really sad. Do you want to talk about it?

— ⚡ —

Catastrophising

Catastrophising is taking something minor and blowing it all out of proportion so that it seems like a calamity. It is imagining the worst possible scenarios, which then trigger fear, which in turn triggers stress, which in turn fuels anger! When we are in our fear and anger, it's impossible to access reason and logic.

Examples of catastrophising language are:

* I can't let him down; he'll be so angry!

* What if I lose my job?
* What if she doesn't like me?
* What if I mess up again?
* Oh my God! What if I can't fix it!

EXERCISE
HOW DO YOU CATASTROPHISE?

Make a list of words or expressions that you find yourself using when you are catastrophising.

• How many of these expressions have been used against you?

• Consider how you could change your language in order to reduce high levels of anxiety and stress in your life. For example:

  * I can't let him down; he'll be so angry! / It's OK to make mistakes; nobody's perfect

  * What if she doesn't like me? / I can't expect everyone to think I'm fabulous.

  * Oh my God! What if I can't fix it! / Let me see if I can fix it before I start to panic.

— ⚡ —

Intellectualising

Intellectualising is over-analysing, dealing with or trying to explain something away through thought or reasoning exclusively, in an attempt to protect ourselves from emotional distress. When we intellectualise, we are in our heads and not in our feelings. In other words, we are emotionally unreachable. We need to learn how to be in both our heads and our hearts at the same time in order to empathise and respond to the emotional needs of others.

Examples of intellectualising language are:

* I just can't understand why I feel this way, can you?
* I try so hard to be normal, but I just keep failing!
* Why am I being so emotional about this?
* I just need to pull myself together and everything will be OK.
* What will the family think if I tell them I'm leaving?
* She is being so emotional; I wish she would just stop!

EXERCISE
HOW DO YOU
INTELLECTUALISE?

Make a list of words or expressions that you find yourself using when you are intellectualising.

* How many of these expressions have been used against you?

* Consider how you could change your language in order to increase your expressiveness and be more in touch with your feelings. For example:

  * Why am I being so emotional about this? / Expressing feelings is healthier than repressing them.

  * I just need to pull myself together. / This is not as serious as I think it is.

  * She is being so emotional; I wish she would just stop! /It's OK for others to express their feelings.

— ⚡ —

Minimising

Minimising is playing down the genuine seriousness of a situation, person or act. The 'poor me' is very good at making minimising comments about themselves to reduce the actual significance of their experiences. By minimising our own experiences, we are actually saying, 'Don't take me, my thoughts, my feelings and my actions seriously.' We may also minimise the significance of other people's experiences.

Examples of minimising language are:

* Surely it doesn't hurt that much.
* Get over it!
* Oh just grow up for God's sake!
* Why can't you just be normal like everyone else?
* Everyone has to do it. Why don't you?

EXERCISE
HOW DO YOU MINIMISE?

Make a list of words or expressions that you find yourself using when you are minimising.

- How many of these expressions have been used against you?

- Consider how you could change your language in order to increase your compassion towards yourself or others and minimise potential animosity. For example:

  * It's not that bad. / You've really struggled through a difficult situation. Well done!

  * Surely it doesn't hurt that much. / This must really hurt. What can I do to help?

  * Everyone has to do it. Why don't you? / You will feel good about yourself by completing the task.

Normalising

Normalising is making something or somebody conform to an artificial standard that you have set. In the context of anger, we may smooth a situation that is actually very abnormal into normality, kidding ourself that aggression and hostility is nothing out of the ordinary when in fact it is extreme.

Examples of normalising language are:

* I just pushed her; it was nothing.
* Everyone shouts at their children.
* My father hit me; that's why I hit her.
* I always behave like that towards him.
* The bruise is nothing really; it will go away.
* It doesn't really hurt, does it?

EXERCISE

HOW DO YOU NORMALISE?

Make a list of words or expressions that you find yourself using when you are normalising.

* How many of these expressions have been used against you?

* Consider how you could change your language in order to have a broader perspective about your own and others' experiences and avoid being judgemental. For example:

  * I just pushed her, it was nothing. / I recognise that my behaviour was inappropriate and that I really frightened her.

  * Everyone shouts at their children. / Shouting is abusive and it scares children.

  * The bruise is nothing really; it will go away. / I am in pain and I need your help.

Personalising

Personalising is intentionally making derogatory remarks or remarks that others will find offensive. It is about seeing yourself as more responsible or involved than you really are. Some of us personalise absolutely everything in our lives and create needless suffering for ourselves.

Examples of personalising language are:

* She's always out to get me.
* How come he always picks on me?
* I'm sure he doesn't like me.
* I'm so stupid; I failed such an easy test.
* What is wrong with me? How come I just don't get it?

EXERCISE
HOW DO YOU PERSONALISE?

Make a list of words or expressions that you find yourself using when you are personalising.

- How many of these expressions have been used against you?

- Consider how you could change your language in order to be more objective and less involved in situations where your involvement is inappropriate. For example:

  * She's always out to get me. / It's OK for her not to trust me.

  * Why does he always pick on me? / I don't have to take what he says or does personally.

  * I'm so stupid; I failed such an easy test. / I'm having a difficult day today; I need to just relax.

— ⚡ —

Generalising

Generalising is believing that your negative experiences apply to all situations. Words such as 'always', 'never', 'everyone', 'nobody', 'all' and 'none' are common when we are generalising.

Examples of generalising language are:

* You always treat me like that.
* You never tell me how pretty I look.
* You should never show your feelings.
* You shouldn't speak to your boss like that.
* Everyone does that.
* You always lie to me.
* You never buy me things.
* Nobody ever listens to me.
* No one takes me seriously.
* My whole life sucks.
* All men want only one thing.

EXERCISE
HOW DO YOU GENERALISE?

Make a list of words or expressions that you find yourself using when you are generalising.

* How many of these expressions have been used against you?

* Consider how you could change your language in order to express less negativity and animosity towards others.

    * You shouldn't speak to your boss like that. / Your boss will understand how upset you are.

    * Nobody ever listens to me. / Please listen when I talk to you.

* All men want only one thing. / I don't like men who take
  advantage of women.

— ⚡ —

As you can see, there are many pitfalls for us to fall into when we
express our anger in an unclean way. I would add to these some
other common forms of distorted thinking.

Mind-reading

We are all very different when it comes to processing our experiences and constructing our own reality. Trying to read someone's
mind or second-guess them is futile and keeps us in a state of anxiety
and uncertainty. It is easier to ask a question than to try anticipate
another person's needs or thoughts. In this way we avoid an
enormous amount of misunderstanding.

Magical thinking

Magical thinking is the belief – against all reasonable expectation –
that things will turn out a particular way. When events do not pan
out as we had hoped, we may feel a great deal of anger (because
our expectations are not being met). This could have been avoided
if our thinking had been more realistic. Had we prepared ourselves
for any one of a range of different outcomes, we would have found
it easier to accept and manage the unwanted outcome with some
equanimity.

Fortune-telling

We are what we think. The belief – despite the fact that we do not
have all the relevant information – that something negative will
happen is often influenced by our past experiences. We may believe

that because a particular thing has happened once, it will happen in the same way again. This is simply not true. Each situation stands alone and needs to be considered on its own merits. Fortune-telling is 'glass half-empty' thinking (as opposed to 'glass half-full'). It's important to keep an open mind rather than attempting to foretell the future. You may just be surprised.

All-or-nothing thinking (polarising)

All-or-nothing thinking is thinking in extremes. There's no middle ground. It's win or lose. The effect of this way of thinking is often to diminish our self-esteem or our opinion of ourselves when we fail. When we consider only total success as acceptable, we are virtually guaranteed to fall short of our own expectations. As a result, we feel bad or stupid. Every time we 'fail' these feelings are reinforced. It's better to have more realistic standards; then we meet them more often, and our self-esteem gets a boost.

This kind of thinking is the domain of the perfectionist. Perfectionists are never satisfied because they set themselves up to fail. This fulfils their deeply-held belief that however hard they try, they are not good enough. Yet if they could drop their polarised thinking and see themselves as others see them, they'd be blown away by their own abilities.

Thinking in 'shoulds'

I always tell participants in my anger management groups to delete the word 'should' from their internal hard drive. 'Shoulds' are self-limiting – rigid demands we make on ourselves, on others and on the world. 'I should ...', 'You should ...' and 'The world should ...' all make the unspoken assumption that if we do not fulfil what the 'should' demands, the results will be disastrous.

Angry and depressed people have many 'shoulds', and these limit their potential. When they don't meet their own unrealistic expectations of themselves, they are kept in a state of frustration and emotional arousal.

Begin today to try to replace the 'shoulds' in your life with other language. You might try:

* I would prefer …
* It's possible to …
* I could try …

A unique form of 'should' is entitlement. Another term for those with a sense of entitlement might be 'special boy' or 'special girl'. These types suffer from the belief that the world owes them a living and that they *should* be favoured above everyone else. They often find themselves at odds with the world and are usually very dissatisfied with their lives.

Oppressive thinking

Every time we compare ourselves unfavourably to others, exaggerating their strengths to the detriment of our own, we internally oppress ourselves, so increasing our feelings of inferiority and inadequacy. Those of us who suffer from low self-esteem and shame are usually extraordinarily skilled at playing this self-destructive game with ourselves.

Another form of thinking oppressively and lowering our self-esteem is feeling envious of or competitive with others. We believe we have to constantly prove to ourselves that we are better than others in order to feel good about ourselves. Alternatively, we may continually put others down.

Of course, distorted thinking does not help us to build our self-esteem and manage our anger. On the contrary, it keeps us in a state of needless suffering and pain.

The task is to become aware of when you employ the types of language and thinking outlined above, so that you can begin to change your thought processes, and recognise and value your own talents and skills. By so doing you will begin to increase your self-esteem. You will find that other people's 'superior' abilities seem less threatening once you can recognise and feel comfortable with your own greatness.

Anger substitutes

It is useful to explore and understand what anger is not, which is directly related to unclean anger and distorted thinking – in other words, what we use to disguise our anger. In his book *Facing the Fire*, John Lee suggests that 'anger equals pain' and that this is why we are afraid to say we are feeling angry. Instead, we express our anger indirectly, via the backdoor or sideways, in order to minimise the fallout if we are imploders or to maximise the fallout if we are exploders.

We use anger substitutes when we are emotionally regressed (we will be discussing regression in detail on page 158), and they are associated with the five anger styles we talked about on pages 120–46. The main anger substitutes are:

* Discounting – *'Don't be so silly'*.
* Judging – *'How dare you behave so badly'*.
* Preaching – *'How many times have I told you how to do this?'*
* Teaching – *'If you had just listened to my advice…'*
* Criticising – *'You should never speak to someone like that'*.
* Demeaning – *'Just shut up or else!'*
* Demoralising – *'You can never stay out of trouble'*.

* Patronising – '*If you had just listened to me in the first place*'.
* Blaming – '*Its your fault that this has happened*'.
* Shaming – '*You such an idiot I cannot believe you did that*'.

We often become so accustomed to speaking in these unhealthy ways rather than being crystal clear about how we feel in the moment. Try reading aloud the following healthy expressions of anger. Then see if you can use them to express your angry feelings in everyday life:

* 'I am feeling angry.'
* 'I feel angry with you.'
* 'I am feeling very angry right now.'
* 'I feel challenged by what you are saying/doing.'

Being direct in this way can feel like an insurmountable challenge, but it is much simpler and healthier to state clearly what we feel. Such statements have a positive effect on both ourselves and others.

EXERCISE
HOW DO YOU EXPRESS YOUR ANGER?

Consider the following questions and write your answers in your journal.

1 How many times have you been able to tell someone in a non-abusive way, 'I am angry with you'? Write a list.

2 How many times have you felt angry with another person and not said anything? Write a list.

3 How many times have you felt angry with another

person and exploded, using abusive and divisive language? Write a list.

Now reflect on the following:

- If you were able to respond to question 1 with examples of occasions when you were able to share your angry feelings with others, you have demonstrated the ability to express clean anger, in which you communicate your feelings in an appropriate, healthy and respectful way.

- If you were able to respond to question 2 with many examples of occasions when you did not share your feelings with others, it is likely that your anger is being expressed in a passive-aggressive manner. It is also likely that you are afraid of your own and others' anger, as well as of the possible fallout from sharing this difficult feeling. But if you go on imploding in this way, it's only a matter of time before you explode – and the result of explosion is usually meltdown in the vicinity. Try to become aware of the words that come out of your mouth when you are being passive-aggressive and see if you can change them to more healthy open expressions of anger.

- If you were able to respond to question 3 with many examples, you have a problem with explosive anger. The next time you feel angry, see if you can remember to stop, think, and take a look at the big picture before you act out. Try simply telling the person that you are angry with them – without the song and dance, without the drama, without the abuse – because, as you already know, when you blow up, you end up feeling shame, remorse and guilt. Consider how wounding your words are and how this kind of behaviour impacts your own personal physical health.

— ⚡ —

Anger as a positive force

When I invite participants in my anger management workshops to explore the idea that anger can be a positive force for change in their lives, they usually look at me as if I am some kind of weirdo! They make objections such as:

* It's because I'm angry that my life is in ruins.
* My anger has destroyed everything that is dear to me.
* The only thing anger is good for is hurting others.
* Being angry is the worst thing that has ever happened to me.
* I would be so happy if I could just get rid of my anger.
* My anger has a life of its own; I have no control over it.
* My anger is like an addiction; it controls me.
* Being angry is like being cursed by God.

My response is to suggest that they consider the concept of determination. We think of determination – or willpower, fortitude, passion, purpose or focus – as good attributes, don't we? And yet the drive that creates determination, that powerful, creative and vital force for making change in our lives, can often be anger!

So let's take a look at how your anger could be an advantage in your life. Your anger can become a tool for transformation.

* Healthy anger often determines whether you should be taken seriously or not.
* Healthy anger gets things done and makes sure they are done well and quickly without fuss or drama.
* Healthy anger can bring issues to a head to be dealt with.
* Healthy anger suggests that you are trying to make an effort to effect change.
* Healthy anger can transform nations – we need look no further than the example set by Nelson Mandela and

Mahatma Gandhi.

* Healthy anger can reshape how you look at the world. It cuts clean through impasses and represents potent and immediate transformation.
* Healthy anger helps us to remain sharp, focused and concentrated.
* Healthy anger gives us a sense of power and control in our own life.
* Healthy anger helps us to face and overcome our fears.
* Healthy anger reduces our sense of inadequacy.
* Healthy anger gives us the energy to stand up for a good cause.
* Healthy anger motivates us to transcend personal limitations and develop self-confidence.
* Healthy anger motivates us to leave abusive situations.
* Healthy anger gains us respect and makes people take notice of us.
* Healthy anger helps us to vent frustrations and release tension in our body.
* Healthy anger protects us.
* Healthy anger helps us to know what we want and need.
* Healthy anger can help us to define who we are in the world in a positive way.
* Healthy anger bonds us with others who are also angry about the same thing.
* With healthy anger, what you see is what you get.

In the men's group I have been running for many years now, when men are angry with each other or with me, they say clearly and respectfully, 'I feel angry with you,' or 'I feel angry at what you have just said' or 'What you said has triggered my anger.' It's clean, simple and to the point. In this particular group, anger is around and is expressed, and once it has been expressed, we move on to other things. Men in this group recognise that it is healthy not only to express their own anger but also to respect other people who are feeling angry and to acknowledge their anger.

The thought of being able to express your anger in this kind of clean, simple way may seem very daunting. In all of my anger management groups, however, once participants have been taught some basic skills, they are able to do this. It is inspiring to see rage-oholics expressing their anger in a healthy way for the first time. This step is liberating, and is the beginning of recognising anger as a transformative tool rather than a weapon of destruction.

EXERCISE
KEY GOALS

In my group work, participants make a list of goals they hope to achieve over the course of their anger management work. These goals can change as time progresses, and usually do, but establishing them is a good way of focusing your energies on what you want to accomplish.

•

Now that you have a good idea of what anger is, how it is triggered, how it impacts your life and the different ways it can find expression, take a moment to make your own list of key goals. This will be helpful as you read through Part Two, in which you will be learning to manage your anger.

— ⚡ —

EXERCISE
REFLECTION

Before you move on to the second part of the book, take
a moment to think about what you have learned from Part
One. Ask yourself:

•

What resonates most for me?

•

Am I ready to start putting some of it into practice
in my life?

— ϟ —

Keep reading – there's more help to come. You're doing great so far!

PART TWO
Managing Your Anger

Courage is more exhilarating than fear and in the long run it is easier. We do not have to become heroes overnight. Just a step at a time, meeting each thing that comes up, seeing it not as dreadful as it appeared, discovering we have the strength to stare it down.

—Eleanor Roosevelt

CHAPTER 5

Facing the Pain

The second part of this book is about application, and part of application is about learning to face our historical hurts, grievances and grudges. We have not only to come to terms with these issues but also to take steps to heal ourselves once and for all.

Past trauma and emotional regression

If you have an anger management problem, you probably try to avoid looking into what lies beneath your anger. You will recall John Lee's statement, 'anger equals pain' (see page 149), and much of this pain is connected to early traumatic experiences. When we come up against an experience in the present that triggers subconscious memories of our early trauma, we become emotionally regressed. In other words, our present reality is conditioned by our memories of our past. Our responses will be motivated by what happened to us in the past, rather by what is actually happening in the present, and may therefore be out of proportion or inappropriate.

It is necessary for anyone who wants to learn how to manage their anger appropriately to understand the genesis of their anger: where the anger comes from, how to tame it and finally how to bring it to resolution. In order to do this, we need to understand the function of trauma and emotional regression in our lives.

Acting out

Acting out is essentially using behaviours that are not helpful, conducive or encouraging to good relationships with others. These include many of the behaviours already discussed in previous chapters. These behaviours all have their roots in the past and are generally associated with trauma and emotional regression. For example, we may revert to a stage of our childhood and completely lose our cool in quite a destructive way.

Acting out is a direct indication that an individual is in an emotionally regressive state and that this behaviour is linked, directly or indirectly, to unfinished business from the past (historic trauma).

It is crucial for individuals with aggressive or passive-aggressive behaviour to understand that almost all their arguments, disputes and confrontations have their origins in the past. If a person has experienced a childhood trauma, however minor it may seem, this trauma will haunt them in the present.

Of course, when we are acting out, we may not be aware that we are engaging in this dysfunctional or self-sabotaging behaviour – until someone else points it out. This may bring us to our senses or it may trigger further hostility and defensiveness.

Participants in my anger management groups are often flabbergasted at how past traumatic events can manifest as angry exchanges in the present. They have never even considered the possibility that the anger they express in the present might have historical associations. They believe that their anger is triggered by present-day interactions only. Becoming aware of the significance of past trauma is often the turning point for them, and they begin to make sense of and understand some of the origins of their emotional difficulties.

Wherever there is a disproportionate amount of anger in response to an event, it is more than likely that unprocessed traumatic experiences from the past are manifesting themselves in the present. The reason why this happens is that our psyche attempts to re-orient us towards optimum health and maximum wholeness by trying to bring closure to unfinished business from the past – even though the events it is reacting to are in the present.

Fred's story

Fred was sitting quietly on the sofa reading the newspaper when his wife, Liz, walked into the room and asked him innocently, 'Darling, did you remember to post the cheque for Clara's school fees?'

Fred went into immediate meltdown, exploded into rage and started hurling abuse at his wife: 'You're always checking up on me! Can't you leave me alone for one second? All I ever get from you is nag, nag, nag. I'm sick and tired of you treating me like a child. Don't you ever stop trying to control me? Do I have to tell you everything I do and don't do? I'm sick and tired of you not trusting me.'

Liz looked at Fred in amazement, wondering what had triggered this hostile and aggressive behaviour. All she had asked was a simple question.

Little did Liz – or Fred – realise that this outburst had been triggered by unconscious (but very much alive) issues for Fred. When Fred was a child he had been asked to leave his school because his father had not paid the fees on time.

Fred was surprised by his own over-reaction and frightened by his angry and aggressive behaviour. He went for a long walk, calmed down and admitted that he had totally over-reacted, but he still felt troubled by the encounter. He decided to discuss this event with his counsellor.

At the counselling session Fred and the counsellor explored

what had led up to Fred's outburst, until finally Fred discovered the fuse that had ignited his anger. He was furious with his father but had never dared express that fury openly. He was too afraid of reprisal, as his father could be a violent man and had occasionally beaten him. Fred went on to share this insight with his wife and it brought them closer together.

Trauma types and symptoms

According to trauma specialist B. A. van der Kolk, 'Trauma is an emotional experience or shock that does not get processed normally and has a lasting psychic effect.' However, there are many different potential causes of this kind of shock. Here are a few of them:

* Serious threat to one's life or emotional integrity
* Serious threat or harm to one's children, partner or other close relatives or friends
* Sudden destruction of one's home or community
* Seeing another person being seriously injured or killed as the result of an accident or physical violence
* Foetal trauma (i.e. trauma that occurs in the womb)
* Birth trauma
* Loss of a parent or close family member
* Illness, high fever, accidental poisoning
* Physical injuries, including falls and accidents
* Sexual, physical or emotional abuse, including abandonment, neglect or beatings
* Witnessing violence
* Natural disasters such as earthquakes, fires or floods
* Certain medical and dental procedures
* Surgery, particularly tonsillectomies and operations for ear problems or for so-called 'lazy eye'

* Anaesthesia
* Prolonged immobilisation – for example, the casting and splinting of the leg or torso during childhood to treat conditions such as turned-in feet or scoliosis

There are very many possible symptoms of trauma. These are some of them:

* Hypervigilance (i.e. being on guard all the time, unable to relax)
* Intrusive imagery or flashbacks
* Extreme sensitivity to light and sound
* Hyperactivity
* Exaggerated emotional and 'startle' responses
* Nightmares and night terrors
* Abrupt mood swings, for example rage reactions, temper tantrums, sudden episodes of shame
* Reduced ability to deal with stress
* Difficulty with sleeping
* Panic attacks, anxiety and phobias
* Mental 'blankness' or 'spaciness'
* Avoidance behaviour (i.e. avoiding certain circumstances that cause you anxiety for reasons you may not even be aware of)
* Attraction to dangerous situations
* Frequent crying
* Exaggerated or diminished sexual activity
* Amnesia and forgetfulness
* Inability to love, nurture or bond with other individuals
* Fears and phobias – of flying, of going crazy, of dying 'before your time'
* Excessive shyness

* Muted or diminished emotional responses
* Inability to make commitments
* Chronic fatigue or very low physical energy
* Immune system problems and certain endocrine problems such as thyroid dysfunction
* Psychosomatic illness, particularly headaches, neck and back problems, asthma, digestive problems, spastic colon and severe premenstrual syndrome
* Depression and feelings of impending doom
* Feelings of detachment, alienation and isolation
* Diminished interest in life
* Behaviours that reflect feelings of powerlessness and helplessness

The trauma cycle

Looking at the theoretical model of the trauma cycle is an excellent way to understand the role of trauma and its cyclical nature in our lives. The stages of the cycle don't necessarily occur in sequence – we may go through one stage and then revert to it later in the trauma process. We can also experience all the stages at the same time. This is often regarded as a mental breakdown, in which the psyche collapses in on itself in order to re-orient itself at a later stage. The stages of the trauma cycle are:

* Triggering
* Re-experiencing the trauma
* Intense emotions (flamboyant behaviour or deafening silence)
* Shame
* Impulsive/compulsive behaviour
* Avoidance and numbness

* Feelings of hopelessness
* Loss of self
* Despair
* Hypervigilance

If you are aware that one or more of these stages is a major factor in your life, I would suggest that you consider working through your issues with a therapist. Working with a trauma therapist might be particularly useful. (See Trauma Incident Recovery in Resources.)

Let's now look at each of the stages in more detail.

Triggering

The triggers for each traumatic experience will be located in the past. Throughout the book I have given a range of examples of what triggers anger, shame, hurt, fear and sadness. It is often the same phenomena that trigger trauma.

Re-experiencing the trauma

On page 46 we explored how the reptilian and mammalian brains play a significant part in reminding us of historical traumatic experiences. We re-experience previous trauma in the present through memory and through physiological responses to present-day events and situations.

Impulsive/compulsive behaviour

Impulsive/compulsive behaviour is usually a response to some form of trauma in a person's past –a natural reaction to the psychological and physiological pain that they are enduring. It is rather like a psychological plaster to cover up the wounding, although in this case the wound does not heal unless psychological work is undertaken to deal with the underlying trauma.

Feelings of hopelessness

Hopelessness is the consequence of an inability to deal with the experience and contents of a trauma and is the sum of a range of negative effects that the trauma is having upon us. Manifest with it is a quiet desperation that resonates throughout our life.

Shame

Shame is a result of traumatic events in childhood and/or the adolescent years. Because of their natural egocentricity, children interpret all events as personal. To a child, everything that happens is about themselves. This means that if things go wrong in the family, the child will believe that it is their fault – and if it is their fault, there must be some thing wrong with them. If these feelings of shame are internalised, the child will become defensive and, more often than not, will project their anger, shame, hurt and fear onto others around them. This causes them further pain, and when this pain becomes intolerable, they may turn to addictions (including compulsive and impulsive behaviour) in order to self-medicate and numb the pain. As the child grows up, the addictions become increasingly sophisticated and may take the form of drug addiction, sex addiction, workaholism, alcoholism and so on. (For more information about shame see pages 176–87.)

Avoidance

Avoidance often takes the form of emotional withdrawal or disengagement in an effort to feel and remain safe. The rationale is that by remaining withdrawn (or numb), we don't have to feel any pain. When pain becomes overwhelming, we leave the painful relationship, job or situation. Avoidant people will frequently take no risks. They are introverted and present themselves as very unthreatening to others, often wearing a blank look or smile. Numbness enables the person to continue functioning in the world – although only just!

Avoidant people are dissociated from their feelings sometimes to the point of sleepwalking their way through life. They are very sensitive to criticism and will withdraw even further in response to it. They are very difficult to reach. The avoidant person's greatest fear is intimacy, because when they wanted closeness in the past, they experienced rejection. Thus numbness has become their defense mechanism against pain and loss.

Loss of self

With loss of self, there is a sense that we are not in the driving seat, that we are not in control of our life. We believe that we don't have access to choices and we are confused about what decisions to take for the best. Loss of self is the result of a sense of despair and help-lessness. We no longer experience ourselves as a whole but as fragmented into millions of pieces. When we experience this loss of self, we seek outside ourselves for self-definition. We look to others for reassurance, to meet our needs and to love us. If they do not do this for us, we become angry or depressed or both. If the underlying unfinished business from our past is not resolved, it may emerge in the form of acting out behaviours, and we may find it impossible to control our rage.

Despair

Despair is brought on by the experience of living in a perpetually pain-filled home, in which no attempt to cope, fix and or oblige succeeds in making things better. Despair comes from feeling that after all it was not meant to work out. It is born out of a profound sense of hopelessness, helplessness and resignation. Despair is associated with a sadness that cannot be penetrated. By other people this sadness may be experienced as overwhelming and scary because of its unplumbable depth. However, despair does have a positive aspect in that when a person hits rock bottom, there is only

one way out, and that is up. By dealing with our despair we can begin
the process of healing.

Hypervigilance

A person who is carrying unresolved trauma in their lives often
becomes hypervigilant both psychologically and physiologically.
They are geared up to react to trauma at all times. Typical charac-
terisitics of hypervigilance are sleep disturbance, restlessness,
difficulty in falling asleep, nightmares, high-content dreams, irri-
tability, anger, outbursts, difficulty in concentrating, exaggerated
startle responses and persistent arousal. When a person is triggered
by unresolved material they will usually resort to expressing their
anger, fear, hurt, sadness or shame in an uncontrolled way, although
they may not be aware of where these strong feelings are coming
from. They will often project these strong feelings onto others as a
way of dealing – or not dealing – with the situation.

The physical effects of trauma

When we are in a state of constant nervous arousal, the central
nervous system sets off a chain of adaptive measures. These are
designed to control and organise the tremendous amount of psychic
and physical energy generated by both the original traumatic event
and the stress response that results. These adaptive measures
function as a safety-valve for the nervous system. Some of them are
triggered shortly after the event; others come into play only over
time. The stages of trauma reaction are:

* Hyperarousal
* Constriction
* Dissociation (including denial)
* Freezing (immobility), associated with the feeling of
  helplessness

Let's now look at each of these stages in more detail.

Hyperarousal

This reaction is rooted in the fight-or-flight mechanism of the central nervous system, which is governed the most primitive part of the brain (see page 47). In reaction to a perceived threat, the body prepares itself either to fight off the threat or flee from it. This involves the following physical reactions:

* Increased heart rate
* Rapid shallow breathing
* Agitation and edginess
* Muscular tension

If we experience this reaction often and over a long period of time, the body never has the chance to relax fully and we leave ourselves open to symptoms such as:

* Difficulty in sleeping
* Muscular tension
* Anxiety attacks

Constriction

When we perceive a threat, the central nervous system acts to ensure that all our efforts can be focused on avoiding or defeating it. The physical effects of this action are known as constriction and include:

* Short rapid breath
* Muscular contraction
* Vascularisation of the muscles (extra blood is directed to the muscles)
* Heightened perceptual awareness, including tunnelling of peripheral vision

These effects are designed to enable us to take action if need be, and they generate an extraordinary amount of energy. Under the influence of constriction, we are able to perform extraordinary feats of strength, such as lifting heavy objects or running long distances.

Dissociation

Dissociation protects us from the impact of increased arousal, severe injury and also from the pain of death. In its mildest form, dissociation is experienced as a form of spaciness. At the other end of the spectrum it might be experienced as multiple personality syndrome. Because dissociation is a breakdown in the continuity of a person's 'felt' sense, it almost always includes distortions of time and perception. A dissociated person may be manic or totally introverted. They are removed from the reality of their own experiences and are unreachable.

Feelings of helplessness

Helplessness is a state of frozenness – rather like being in suspended animation. Think of the rabbit in the headlights; this is helplessness. Helplessness is a biological response to the experience of an overwhelming threat in which the central nervous system, guided by the 'old' brain (see page 46) goes into complete shutdown. The 'old' brain is the storehouse of memory. When we encounter a situation that triggers memories of the original threat, we automatically respond as if to that original threat.

Trauma can occur without our even being aware that it is traumatic. Indeed, we often dismiss traumatic events as 'nothing' or as of no consequence really – 'no big deal'. In this way we normalise our painful experiences. For example, clients often describe to me childhood experiences of being left alone somewhere for hours – or at least what seems like hours. They cry and cry, and no one comes. Finally, they fall asleep from exhaustion. When this kind of trauma is described in a matter of fact way, I hear alarm bells ringing. This kind of experience often triggers an incomplete physiological response, suspended by fear. These symptoms will not go away until the emotion surrounding the original trauma is discharged, brought to a complete resolution and integrated.

The detour process

As I have already mentioned, you know when you are in an emotionally regressed state when your anger is disproportionate to the circumstance or event. Your body displays stress signals – your hands sweat, your heart pounds, your head feels as if it's going to explode, your hands curl into a fist, your knees shake, your lips quiver and your throat contracts. You have moved into an overwhelm position.

At this point you will probably do everything possible to try to regress the other person. In other words, you will say and do things designed to hurt. The subtext to this dangerous and toxic game is 'If I can hurt you, it means I have won this round.' Like misery, regression just loves company, and the situation soon degenerates into a negative spiral in which each person tries to regress the other further. In your state of regression you are unable to be fully in the present. You will not be able to stick to the issues at hand, and the situation will get out of control. Do you recognise some of this behaviour in your more fractious relationships?

This game will continue until such time as one person decides to discontinue playing, recognising that it has become dangerous, competitive and meaningless, and that it can only lead to both of you feeling hurt, resentful and possibly bitter.

The task is to recognise these symptoms and pull yourself out of the combat zone at the earliest stage possible. This is much safer for all parties concerned. You do this by stating that you are leaving and explaining why. For example, you might say, 'I can see where this argument is leading and I am not willing to go there. I need some time out and will continue this conversation when I have calmed down.' Be careful to say this in a way that will not fuel the regression of the other person. Make sure your tone is reassuring rather than blaming or shaming and that you commit to discussing the issue at hand at a later stage. If possible, call someone in your support network to help you come out of the state of regression and find clarity. It's only in the realms of adulthood that we can create safety for ourselves and those around us.

The fact that you are in a regressed state means that you have almost certainly touched on historical unresolved traumatic material. This means that there is something in your past emotional experience that is calling out for your attention. The detour method offers you the opportunity to bring this material to resolution once and for all. Bringing closure to traumatic issues from your past means that these issues no longer hijack you in the present. In other words, once you resolve the issue you will not be triggered in the same way in the future, and your reactions will not be so extreme. By following the steps of the detour method you will be able to bring yourself back to your adult state and unearth a wealth of information about your needs.

The detour process was designed by John Lee, author of *Grow Yourself Up Again*. It is highly effective, and I would certainly recommend that you buy a copy of Lee's book. The following is just a brief description of the process. It is necessary that you have an anger buddy to take you through the process and to provide a safe space. You should arrange to meet with them as soon as you find yourself in a state of regressive anger – with signs such as shaking, heat, thumping heart and so on. If you meet face to face, call them.

You need to teach your anger buddy the basic detour method model before you actually need to use the process. They should know the following:

• *They need to be able to give you as much time as you need*
When you contact your anger buddy, be clear about how much of
their time you need (the process will usually take only ten to
fifteen minutes) and ask them if they are able to give it to you. If
they are unable to give you their time on this occasion, either ask
if you can call them back when they are less busy (but make sure
you do call them back) or call another member of your support
network.

• *They need to give you their full attention*
They should be aware that part of giving full attention is
remaining silent and listening, without interrupting or expressing
an opinion – no matter how well they think they know you.

• *They need to be empathetic*
Your anger buddy must keep their heart open and avoid
judgement, criticism and advice.

• *They need to be aware that you may want to be touched or held
as part of the process but that they should ask your permission
before doing so*
During the process you may feel the need to be held or touched in
a particular way, for example by having your hand held. However,
your anger buddy must ask you first if you want to be touched or
held, and not assume that it's ok to do so. Once you have given
them your permission, it is your responsibility to tell them how
you would like to be touched and where. Be very specific about
what kind of touch you want, for example to be held more tightly
or more gently.

• *They need to be able to support you in emotional release work.*
Emotional release work may include hitting or shouting into a

pillow, twisting a towel, punching a punch-bag, tearing up an old telephone book, chopping wood, dancing to loud music, screaming and so on. (For more about emotional release work see page 181.) The intention is to enable you to express what has been repressed or buried. Trauma exists because we were not able to express ourselves fully at the time of the original event, so it is important that you give yourself permission finally to complete this process.

The process

There are six stages in the detour process. All the support person has to do is ask the questions listed below and listen to your answers, allowing each answer to come to a natural end before asking you the next question.

1 Anger buddy: 'Tell me what has happened?'

This question refers to the present-day incident.

For example:

You: *He started to scream and shout at me and call me names. I just lost it and went berserk and started throwing punches at the wall to let all my anger out.*

2 Anger buddy: 'How old do you feel right now?'

This question refers to the age you have regressed to.

For example:

You: *I think I feel … about … seven or eight years old.*

3 Anger buddy: 'What happened when you were — years old?'

For example:

You: *I remember sitting in the living room and my father and mother were shouting at each other. My mother turned to my father and threw a dish on the floor and my father*

*went ballistic. He saw me out the corner of his eye and
shouted at me to go up to my room. I refused, and he
grabbed me by the scruff of my neck and threw me out of
the living room and slammed the door shut. I heard my
mother screaming for me to help her, but I was locked out. I
went up to my bedroom and locked my door and cried
myself to sleep. The next morning the police arrived and
took my father away ...*

**4   Anger buddy: 'If you could turn back the clock now,
what would you like to say or do? Say it now ... ... Say
it louder.'**

For example:

You: *I hate you daddy ...*

Support person: *Say it louder.*

You: *I hate you daddy!*

Support person: *Say it louder.*

You: *I HATE YOU DADDY! I hate it when you hurt mummy
and me!*

Support person: *Say it louder this time.*

You: *Don't hurt me!*

Support person: *Say that louder.*

You: *Don't you hurt me, you bully! Don't you ever hurt me
again, you bully! You will never, ever hurt me again!*

5   Anger buddy: 'Are you feeling any better?'

For example:

You: *Yes, I am ... thank you.*

If you are not feeling any better, your anger buddy should ask if
there is anything else you need to say, and if there is, they should
facilitate you to say it, following the protocol in point 4. This dialogue

should continue until such time as you really do feel better. This is a very important part of the process, so be sure that you say all you need to say at this stage. You will only be able to move out of your regressed state once you feel genuinely OK. Don't cheat yourself, continue until you really do feel better.

6 Anger buddy: 'Thank you.'

Allowing yourself to express your hurt and anger and being witnessed in this place is an example of healthy aggression (assertiveness). By returning to the historical place to which you have regressed and unfreezing that child once and for all, you help that repressed part of you to regain its voice, dignity and self-respect. In this way you can heal yourself and continue with your life in a more whole and functional way.

Preverbal trauma detour method

It sometimes happens that when it comes to expressing what you want to say, there are simply no words. In this case it is likely that your trauma was experienced at an age before you learned to speak fluently. However, your body will certainly remember the experience and may want to do or act something out. If this is the case, your anger buddy should follow these steps:

In this case follow these steps:

1 **Anger buddy:** *'Tell me what has happened.'*

2 **Anger buddy:** *'How old do you feel right now?'*

3 **Anger buddy:** *'What would your body like to have done back then? ... ... Let your body express it now.'*

4 **Anger buddy:** *'Are you feeling any better?'*

5 **Anger buddy:** *'What did you need at that time? ... ... What do you need now?'*

6 **Anger buddy:** *'Thank you.'*

After witnessing an individual completing the detour process on one of my anger management programmes, one participant told the group, 'I've been looking for a miracle cure for anger; I think I have just found it.' It struck me at the time how true this statement was. The detour process really is a miracle cure – the key to bringing our anger under control and expressing it proportionately. I have witnessed it many times and continue to be astounded by its effectiveness.

Shame

Many of those who have attended my anger management courses have quickly learned that they have not only an anger management problem but also a shame management problem. Their anger serves as a defence against their feelings of shame. Thus in order to deal with the anger it becomes imperative to descend into the depths of their shame and face what lies there.

We can view the word 'shame' as being made up of two parts: sh (= 'shhh', to keep quiet/be silent) + ame (= âme, the French for 'soul'). Thus shame may be regarded as the silencing of the soul.

By not giving voice to our soul, we attempt to limit our need for emotional nourishment. We do this because we want to be seen as all OK, all right, fine – and in extreme cases as perfect. But by curbing ourselves in this way, in fact we restrict and hurt ourselves.

We have already seen how how self-defensive anger arises as a response to shame (see pages 66–70). Here, we will be discussing shame in a little more depth. First of all let's take a look at the difference between healthy shame and toxic shame.

Healthy shame

In his excellent book, *The Shame that Binds You*, John Bradshaw defines healthy shame as 'an emotional signal that we have made and will make mistakes'. According to Bradshaw, 'Healthy shame gives us permission to be human.'

We all make mistakes; they are part of the human condition and the means by which we all learn. The embarrassment or guilt that they may cause us are signs of our limitations as human beings. When we are experiencing healthy shame, we know that it's OK to make mistakes, get things wrong, to mess up, to disappoint others and ourselves – and afterwards to dust ourselves off and begin again.

The ability to acknowledge our humanity is vital to our emotional and spiritual wellbeing. If we are hell-bent on being perfect, on always doing the 'right' thing, we will find ourselves in constant conflict with the reality of our own inherent imperfection. Recognising our limitations and surrendering to them is part of what it means to be human, and this process can be profoundly transformative. If we live our lives preoccupied with measuring up to others, we are creating perpetual – and needless – suffering for both ourselves and those around us.

Surrendering to who we are – accepting that we make mistakes but are not a mistake – is crucial in making our relationship with shame a healthy one.

Toxic shame

In *The Shame that Binds You*, John Bradshaw describes toxic shame as 'no longer an emotional signal to our limits of being human'; instead it is 'a state of being, a core identity, a core wounding to the soul'. According to Bradshaw, 'Toxic shame gives you a sense of worthlessness, failure and being less than human.'

Toxic shame is a rupture within the self, like internal bleeding. When we experience toxic shame, we will guard against the excruciating pain of exposing the core of who we are to others, because we believe that in our core we have failed. We distrust our own deepest self and thus our own experiences, and we feel compelled to be perfect in what we say, do and feel – at whatever cost. When we are caught in our own toxic shame, we are relentlessly hard on ourselves.

Some of the statements that accompany toxic shame are:

* I am a mistake
* I am flawed and defective as a human being
* I am an object and cannot be trusted
* I cannot trust myself
* I am absent and empty inside

Toxic shame is self-perpetuating, in that we feel ashamed about feeling so much shame. As a result, we tend to isolate ourselves. Most of us will admit to guilt, hurt or fear before they will own up to feeling shame.

In order to avoid facing our own shame, we may use behaviours such as:

* Perfectionism
* Striving for control and power
* Anger, aggression, hostility, resentment and rage
* Criticism and blame
* Judging and moralising
* Self-contempt and contempt for others
* Patronising behaviour
* Caretaking and rescuing (helping other people)
* Envy and jealousy
* Indifference
* People-pleasing and being likeable at all costs (nice-guy persona)

John Bradshaw describes the shame-bound person as dwelling 'in the depths of a dark hostile forest, to keep us protected from a world which we perceive and experience as threatening and dangerous to our whole being'. This forest keeps us safe – or so we like to think – but, alas, every tree in the forest has a 360-degree mirror wrapped around it, so that wherever we look, we see what we believe to be our own imperfections and shortcomings. Hiding in the forest is futile, because we cannot hide from our own incessantly shaming internal self-images.

As long as our shame remains hidden, we can do nothing about it. In order to deal with it, we have to embrace it. We have to familiarise ourselves with the territory of the forest so that we can bring shame within our emotional control. This is especially the case if you have been using anger as a defense mechanism against the sting of shame.

Focusing on where your shame originates from and how it became established in your life in the first place is as important as working on your anger – in fact, you need to recognise that, like twins, shame and anger go hand in hand.

If you suffer from toxic shame, you can do yourself a huge favour by buying a copy of John Bradshaw's definitive book on the subject, *The Shame that Binds You*. By following the guidelines it lays out, you can set yourself on the road to emotional recovery from this crippling condition.

Where does shame come from?

Usually, it is our primary caretakers, our parents, older or younger siblings, grandparents, relatives, playground bullies and even teachers who, unknowingly, condemn us to the belief that we are intrinsically flawed and that if we allowed others to know this, they would reject or abandon us.

As we discussed on page 165, children are essentially egocentric. In other words, they naturally believe that everything that happens is about them. Through their magical thinking, children come to believe that they have the power to change external events. They quite naturally create fantasies and magical stories about their parents. These fantasies help them to feel safe and secure – even if in reality they experience life as dangerous and their parent(s) as scary, hostile and unpredictable. Sigmund Freud coined the term 'fantasy bond' for the connection that children make with their parents through these stories. He suggests that the fantasy bond is the first major defence mechanism we use to protect ourselves from emotional pain. In order to keep the fantasy bond intact, we generate inaccurate negative information, thoughts, ideas and fantasies against ourselves. To protect the image of our parents, we may remain imprisoned in the resulting shame for many years.

John's story

When John began to explore the question of where his shame came from, he could not quite put his finger on it. He could not remember his parents ever behaving in a shaming way towards him, nor his siblings or cousins. It was while he was attending a leadership weekend that his insight came. He suddenly connected with a memory of his grandfather, and a surge of feelings rose up within him.

In the group process John asked someone to represent his grandfather. He got hold of a baseball bat and a big cushion so that he could safely focus his anger and just let rip. As he began to enter into the emotional experience of his memory, feelings that he had been holding about his grandfather for years started to emerge. He unleashed outrage over how his grandfather used to compare John to his younger cousin, setting up the two cousins in competition against each other, and how he used to mock and criticise John in front of his parents and family.

As John accessed and expressed his rage in a controlled

environment, the toxicity of his shame began to melt away like snow and he felt lighter, happier and more relaxed. As a result, he went on to realise that he didn't have to take criticisms in his life so personally, and he became less reactive to situations.

EXERCISE
RELEASE YOUR SHAME

Once you have identified who has shamed you in your life, it is important that you express your rage at them in a healthy way. In order to do this, you will need one or two witnesses – anger buddies from your support network. If you are to overcome your shame, it is vitally important that it is witnessed, because the very crux of shame is that it does not want to be seen. The witnesses also hold a safe, contained space for you to reveal your pain and release your anger. Expressing frozen rage is a healthy activity, but it needs to be controlled and supported by those working with you. On your own part, you should be mindful not to hurt yourself or your anger buddies.

•

Gather together with your witnesses and explain to them the purpose of this exercise and what they need to do.

•

Place a baseball bat or tennis racket and a very large cushion or punch bag in a space large enough for you to really take a swing at the cushion without injuring anyone or damaging anything. Place a chair in front of you, about 120 centimetres (4 feet) away.

•

Imagine the person or persons who have shamed you sitting on the chair in front of you. If it helps, ask one of your anger buddies to sit on the chair to represent this person. Take as long as you need to connect with the emotions surrounding your memories of this person.

•

Now grip the bat with both hands, focusing on your anger. Bring the bat over the top of your head and then down on the cushion. Let rip for about 30 seconds, experiencing what it's like to access the power of your frozen rage. This is about expressing healthy aggression, which will help to unfreeze those frozen parts of you.

•

Tell the person in front of you what you resent about them. For each thing you resent, bring the bat down on the cushion with all your might. Make sure you work through all your resentments. Examples of resentments might be:

* I resent you for mocking me.

* I resent you for putting me down.

* I resent you for patronising me.

* I resent you for lying to me.

•

Pause for a few moments. The next stage in the process is to make some demands of the person in the chair. Again, as you make each demand, bring the bat over your head with all the force you can muster. Examples of demands might be:

* I demand that you look at me.

* I demand that you never touch me again.

* I demand that you hold me.

* I demand that you love me.

* I demand that you leave me alone.

•

Once you have completed the above steps, you can – if you want – tell the person or persons who shamed you what you appreciate about them. It is quite possible that at this point you may not want to appreciate them, and this is fine. Sometimes it's important to allow the anger to 'settle' first, and this may take a couple days or weeks. Examples of appreciations might be:

* I appreciate you giving me life.

* I appreciate your humour.

* I appreciate you holding me.

* I appreciate how you treated Mum.

•

If an anger buddy is representing the person or persons who shamed you, you should now tell them, 'You are not – (name of person they are representing), you are my friend, – (name).' They should say in return, 'I am not – (name of person they are representing), I am your friend, – (name).' It is imperative that you include this step.

•

This process is a very powerful way of unfreezing shame. As a result of undertaking it, you will probably find that you become happier and more relaxed, and less invested in what other people think of you.

— ϟ —

The only way out is through

Unfortunately, there are no shortcuts when it comes to transforming our shame. All our attempts to bypass and suppress it are ineffectual in the long term. Embracing our shame involves pain, and pain is what we try to avoid. However, the more we run away

from our shame, the more intensely we experience it. The following
are ways in which you can own and externalise your shame, thus
ridding yourself of it once and for all:

* Be honest about how you feel and share your feelings with
  others whom you feel close to and safe with. This will give
  you the courage to deal with people who feel less safe – and
  survive the ordeal.
* Use people in your support network to explore some of the
  issues you are ashamed about in your life. This is an
  excellent way to build a safe bridge between you and
  others. You could also explore these issues with a therapist,
  a therapy group or close friends. We need people to witness
  our shaming experiences.
* Write about historical shaming experiences in your anger
  management journal. This will help to externalise them. It
  will also help to clarify any fears you may have of rejection
  and abandonment as a result of admitting to your shame.
  By really connecting with these feelings we are able to
  bring them to rest.
* Develop a dialogue with your inner child, with the intention
  of building a conscious rapport. The inner child is the
  internalised child part of us that seldom gets any of our
  attention. When our inner child does not get our attention,
  just like any other child, it will do what it can to attract it.
  (To find out more on inner child work, read John
  Bradshaw's *Homecoming* – the best book on the subject of
  inner-child work I have ever read.)
* Learn to recognise the parts of yourself that you have split
  off and consigned to your shadow. Begin the process of
  embracing and integrating these aspects of yourself by
  talking about them.
* Use affirmations as a way of embracing those parts of

yourself that have disgusted you. Look and tell yourself, 'I love myself for ...', 'I think I am great because ...' Spend five minutes doing this. Even if this feels inaccurate, act as if it is true.

* Write about traumatic memories and find effective ways of healing them, for example by writing or talking about them.

* Learn to recognise the negative, self-judgemental voices in your head and replace them with nurturing, positive ones. Negative voices keep our shame spirals in operation.

* Become sensitized and aware of certain interpersonal events that are triggers for your shame and be creative how you deal with these situations.

* Learn to deal with critical and shaming people by practising assertiveness techniques such as those described on pages 149–51 and not taking things personally.

* Practise empathy and compassion towards yourself and have the courage to be imperfect.

* Use prayer and/or meditation to create an inner place of silence in which you are centred and grounded.

EXERCISE
SHAME ASSESSMENT

This exercise is designed to help you to begin to think about the role of shame in your life. You will probably score highly in some areas and low in others.

On a scale of 0–10 (0 being do not agree at all and 10 being agree completely), rate yourself on each of the following statements:

1 I worry about how I look.

2 I am concerned about what others think of me.

3 When I say what I really think, I'm embarrassed later.

4   I feel self-conscious when I'm with others.

5   I have trouble handling criticism.

6   I'm afraid I'll be humiliated in front of others.

7   I expect others to see my flaws.

8   I notice my faults daily.

9   When other praise me, it's hard for me to believe what they're saying.

10 I don't think I'm as good as other people I know.

11 I feel ashamed of the way other people in my family act.

12 Sometimes I feel ashamed and I don't know why.

13 I worry about what I'll do wrong.

14 I hate being evaluated, even though I know I have done a good job.

15 I feel ashamed just being around somebody who's acting dumb.

16 I am a perfectionist in everything I do.

17 I am shy and blush easily.

18 I like the world to see me as perfect, sorted, in control, integrated, OK and good at what I do.

19 I'm a nice guy/girl.

20 I want the world to see me as a nice person.

If you have scored yourself highly for more than 15 of the statements, you definitely need to do some of the shame work outlined above.

If you have scored yourself highly on ten to fifteen of the statements, your relationship with shame is less toxic, but it would benefit you to undertake some shame work as described above.

If you have scored yourself highly on five to ten of the statements, you have a slight amount of shame and should do some work around the specific issues that you feel ashamed about. You might try exploring them with an anger buddy.

If you scored yourself highly on less than five of the statements, you are fortunate enough not to suffer significantly from toxic shame and can move on to the work in the next section.

— ⚡ —

EXERCISE
EXPLORING THE ROLE OF SHAME IN YOUR LIFE

Answer the questions below, writing your responses in your journal.

- What is the shame that binds you?

- How did it get established in your life?

- What happens to healthy shame in the process? (Healthy shame is our ability to recognise that we have limitations, that we are not perfect, that we make mistakes and that's OK – it's not the end of the world.)

Now show your answers to two or three people you trust. Discuss your answers with them in detail.

— ⚡ —

Owning your shadow

As we learnt on page 72, the shadow is those parts of ourselves that remain hidden, denied and repressed. From the perspective of anger management, the shadow is the part of us that acts out in an out-of-control manner in response to certain situations. When our shadow is activated, we can become very dangerous to both ourselves and others.

Dr Carl Jung suggested that we need to develop a healthy relationship with the shadow aspects of our psyche in order to understand and accept all of who we are. When we consign parts of ourselves that we fear or are ashamed of to the shadow, they don't go away; they merely become part of our subconscious, and thus out of our conscious control.

In *The Little Book of Shadows* Robert Bly describes the shadow as a little sack that we are born with on our back. As we grow up, every time we are told 'Don't do that!', 'Behave yourself!', 'Stop annoying your mother!', 'Grow up!', 'Stop crying!', 'Shut up!', 'Pull yourself together!', 'Don't ever speak like that again!' ... etc., another item goes into the sack. By the time we reach adulthood, most of us have sacks filled to bursting point.

We deal with feelings of anger and shame by repressing them – in other words, we throw them into the little sack, where they turn into self-judgements, self-criticisms and eventually self-loathing. As such, they cloud our perception of the world and ultimately turn into judgements and criticisms of others. When the sack becomes just too heavy to shoulder, our anger starts to burst forth uncontrollably. All this anger has to go somewhere, and because we have repressed its legitimate targets, we turn it onto other people. This is known as shadow projection.

The rule of thumb I use is 'If you spot it, you got it.' In other words, when you find yourself reacting to what someone else is saying or doing, it is probably because they are touching on something you have stuffed into your shadow sack.

The golden shadow

We mentioned the golden shadow on page 73. Now let's look at it in
more detail. In essence, the golden shadow contains that part of us
that needs to be celebrated, the genius inside us. According to Jung,
a remarkable 85 per cent of our shadow is pure gold!

So why would we repress that within us which is gold? In order
to fit in and be loved. Consider this. Our parents, primary carers,
grandparents, teachers and anyone else responsible for our
upbringing all have their own shadows. If they see us expressing
certain behaviours that they are uncomfortable with, they instinc-
tively want to shut them down. And sometimes these behaviours
involve our exuberance, our joy, our creativity. If you see someone
behaving in a manner that scares you, do you not react in a similar
way?

We may interpret these responses in a variety of ways, for
example:

* Don't be you
* Don't succeed
* Don't grow up
* Don't feel
* Don't think
* Don't exist
* Don't be a child
* Don't be important
* Don't belong
* Don't be close
* Don't be well
* Don't be sane
* Don't create

Thus we came to believe that in order to belong, to feel safe and protected, we have to squash ourselves into shapes and forms that do not threaten our carers. This may mean diminishing our imagination, brilliance and own innate greatness in order to be 'OK' according to the criteria of the system we were born into.

Christopher's story

Christopher had always wanted to write a play. He had conceived this play in his mind hundreds of times, but each time he actually put pen to paper, he heard the voices of his father and mother telling him, 'You'll never be successful as a writer; when you grow up, get a real job like your brother.' As a result, Christopher disowned his own potential. Over many years, he conditioned himself to believe that his father and mother knew him better than he did.

Then one day, after years of trying and failing to write his play, Christopher decided to challenge his parents' view. He recognised that he had a talent and he was determined to put it to good use. He wrote a 500-word synopsis for his wife, Jenny, to read. Jenny was blown away by Christopher's talent. She gave the synopsis to a friend's husband who worked in the theatre, and before he knew it, Christopher had a commission to write the play. The play was then passed on to an up-and-coming director, who agreed to direct it at the Edinburgh Fringe Festival. To Christopher's astonishment the play was so successful that it eventually toured the whole of England.

EXERCISE
CHASE THE GOLDEN SHADOW

In your journal, make a list of everything you are not happy with about yourself, for example: 'I am unfit,' 'I am irresponsible with money,' 'I smoke.'

•

Now make a list of everything you are happy with about yourself, for example: 'I play beautiful music,' 'I am a loyal friend,' 'I am a good cook.'

•

Count the entries on your 'not happy with' list. Count the entries on your 'happy with' list. Which is the longest?

•

If your 'happy with' list is longest, congratulations. If your 'not happy with' list is longest, you are typical of most of us. When we are in the grip of our shadow, we are inclined to focus more on our weaknesses than on our strengths. In order to heal our wounds, we need not only to reclaim our dark elements but also to celebrate the golden aspects of ourselves that we have banished, for it is these golden aspects that contain our bliss.

— ⚡ —

Origins of the shadow: the fantasy bond

The fantasy bond is a brilliant concept that Freud came up with to explain the origins of the shadow. To understand it, we need to remember that parents are the most important factors in a child's world. Without the protection of a parent, the human infant is completely helpless. It is therefore crucial for children to know that they belong, that they are loved and protected, and that they can trust their parents completely. If their experience shows them that none of the above is true, then they have to fantasise that it is true in order to avoid suffering an unbearable existential terror.

In his book, *The Fantasy Bond*, Robert Firestone defines this bond as the illusion of connectedness that an infant creates with its primary carer whenever its emotional needs are threatened. Children are equipped with the innate ability to protect their conscious awareness in this way. They do this automatically and unconsciously, and it is the unconscious quality of these defences that makes them so potentially damaging. Because no caretaker or parent is perfect, we all develop fantasy bonds to some degree or other.

Growing up and leaving the family home involves the ability to relinquish the infantile bond with our parents or carers. According to Fritz Perls, the founder of Gestalt Therapy, in order to become an adult we have to learn to tolerate being alone, and this means shattering the illusion of the idealised parents. However, this takes courage and a leap of faith, and not all of us are able to negotiate the transition successfully. The more emotionally deprived or abandoned we feel, the more compelling the fantasy bond will be and the more we will tend to adhere to an idealised version of the parents and family.

What I make up about you

So now let's take a look at how the shadow gets played out in our daily lives.

In confrontational situations, we tend to make a lot of assumptions without any reality-testing, i.e. asking the other person for clarification. Rather than seeking to gain a fuller understanding of exactly what they mean and what they need, we impose our own world view, our own assumptions, onto them, believing we know what they are thinking or feeling. You have probably been on the receiving end yourself, so you will know how it makes you feel. This is regressive behaviour, linked to unresolved traumas from our childhood, and its intention is to regress the other person too.

When we make up things about other people and tell them what they mean or what they are really trying to say, we are engaged in projection. We do this all the time. Imagine, for example, that a colleague is angry with you. But instead of owning their own anger, they project it onto you and say that *you* are angry with *them*. They do this, without asking you how you feel, what you think or what's going on for you.

We do this because we are afraid of facing the truth about ourselves – afraid to own up to ourselves that, for example, we are angry. We do it in order to justify and affirm our own dysfunctional behaviour.

It is part of human nature to attempt to protect the ego in this way. The ego hates to see itself as 'less than'. It cannot tolerate being wrong and will not accept that it has shortcomings. Nevertheless, it is our responsibility to become aware of when this process is going on and to halt it. Once we are conscious that we are projecting, we can change our language to reflect the fact that *we* are responsible for our own feelings, thoughts and behaviour.

The next time you are in conflict with another person, try using the words 'What I make up about you ...' By using this phrase you are taking responsibility rather than laying blame, and so changing the nature of the interaction between you and the other person. You will probably find that they respond to you much more positively. Here are a few examples:

Rather than saying: 'You are uncaring and selfish.'

Say: 'What I am making up about you at the moment is that you are uncaring and selfish, and as a result I find myself becoming very angry with you.'

Rather than saying: 'You make me so angry!'

Say: 'What I make up about you is that the hurt I feel is a result of what you are doing to me.'

Rather than saying: 'I am always late because of you!'

Say: 'What I make up about you is that when I am late it is your fault rather than my responsibility.'

Rather than saying: 'I try so hard but you never listen to me!'

Say: 'What I make up about you is that you never listen to me even though I try hard to make you.'

EXERCISE
WHAT I MAKE UP ABOUT YOU

Make a list of five grievances that you have towards a person or persons. Now use the structure below to rephrase your grievances in a self-responsible way.

Rather than saying:

....

....

Say: What I make up about you is

....

....

— ⚡ —

Take some time out now to consider what you have learnt from this chapter. Give yourself some praise for having come this far in your journey towards understanding and managing your anger. Really appreciate the effort you are putting in to help yourself overcome your difficulties. You are taking positive steps towards personal growth and fulfilment. Thank yourself!

CHAPTER 6

Expressing Anger Safely

In previous chapters you have discovered some of the many underlying causes of anger. Hopefully, this will have given you an insight into the reasons for your behaviour and an incentive for changing it. I'm sure that by now you have realised that this involves ongoing work and will require your commitment to the best of your ability on a daily basis. Now let's take this a step further and look at some safe alternative ways of expressing your anger.

Four powerful steps to controlling anger

Each of the following steps will help you to see your anger in perspective. It will also help you to be clear about what is yours and what is not yours. Once you have this kind of clarity in relation to the trigger for your anger, you will find that the situation is not insurmountable. Your ability to control your anger will grow as you get the hang of the four steps. Indeed, by following them you can make your anger a powerful tool for change.

Step one: tune in to the primary source of your anger and clarify your wants, needs and position

When you find yourself in conflict with someone, ask yourself the following questions:

* TRIGGERS: What is it about the situation that triggers my anger
* ISSUES: What are the real issues here?
* ACCOMPLISH: What do I want to accomplish?
* NEEDS: What needs of mine are not being met?
* RESPONSIBILITY: Who is responsible for what?
* CHANGE: What specifically do I want to change?
* ACCEPT: What am I willing to accept about my own behaviour?
* SHADOW: What part of my Shadow is being played out here?
* BOUNDARIES: What are the things that I will subject myself to and the things that I cannot subject myself to without compromising my own integrity?

Step two: learn some simple key communication skills

These are skills such as:

* Anger by appointment only (see page 252)
* No blaming or shaming
* Listening carefully while someone is speaking (you may learn something) – no interruptions!
* Asking the other person to just listen while you are speaking
* Hearing and understanding rather than trying to convince the other person of what is fair or right
* Making 'I' statements – for example 'I feel angry', 'I feel scared', 'I feel hurt'
* Taking responsibilty for your actions, thoughts, feelings, behaviour and attitude

* Owning up to your own shadow projections and
  dysfunctional behaviour
* Recognising that the enemy is within and is not the person
  with whom you are in conflict

Step three: become the silent witness and disrupt counter-productive patterns of behaviour

You can do this by taking the following measures:

* Standing back and being self-observant and self-aware
* Being flexible and empathetic and staying calm
* Taking a deep breath and remaining grounded in the here
  and now
* Stopping, thinking and taking a look at the big picture
* Asking yourself what you can take responsibility for in this
  dispute
* Taking responsibility for all your own feelings
* Seeing the quarrel as a destructive game – and making a
  mature choice not to play it

Step four: expect resistance to change and anticipate reactions from others

Be aware that:

* Some people are invested in you remaining exactly the way
  you are
* The anger you are expressing may not always be just for
  yourself – ask yourself who it is for. It may be the
  unexpressed anger of your mother, father, sibling ... etc.
* We often resist making the changes that we ourselves
  actually desire
* Ask this key question: is this about me, you or us? This
  simple question will help you to clarify and define your own
  personal and emotional boundaries

Robert's story

Robert is aware that he has been angry since birth. Every time he finds himself in confrontational situations – no matter how minor – he will blow. One way or another, he always finds an excuse to lose it.

In our work in therapy together, we explored whether there was a way in which he could control his anger, or at least express his feelings without making judgments or being abusive to others. However, Robert found it impossible to see another way, because his fundamental belief was that life was a battlefield and in order to be on top he had to make sure that no one – absolutely no one – got the upper hand. In fact, he described himself as a loaded cannon just waiting to go off.

I decided to go through each of the four steps systematically with Robert, asking him to identify examples relating to angry confrontations that he created for himself. Firstly, I asked him to tune in to the primary source of his anger and clarify his wants, his needs and his position regarding the issue in conflict. Secondly, we explored simple key communication skills that he could apply in challenging situations. Thirdly, I suggested that he become a fly on the wall (in other words, be the silent witness) and in so doing see if he could identify the disruptive, counter-productive patterns of behaviour that he demonstrated in these conflicted situations. Finally, we explored his own and others' resistance to change and looked at how he could prepare himself for reactions from others as he began the process of not engaging in the conflict and drama that he was used to creating in his life.

As each week went by, we further deconstructed the confrontations Robert had created and he slowly began to see that he had choices – that he could change and that the world was only as hostile as he considered it to be.

When the time came for Robert to end his one-to-one-work
with me, he said, 'I remember when you told me that the
enemy was within. I didn't quite understand that at the time,
but now I do. Learning these four basic steps to controlling
anger has enabled me to change my life.'

Six key components for resolving conflict

Having considered the four steps to controlling anger, we will move
on to look at the skills needed to resolve conflict. Conflict is painful
and difficult. Although we cannot negotiate life without engaging
with it, we can certainly take measures to limit the damage it causes.
Conflict can also teach us an enormous amount about ourselves and
those we are in relationship with. It bares our soul, and, if managed
skillfully, can bring us closer to others.

This easy-to-use method will help you to bring self-supportive
and emotionally satisfying resolution to even the most difficult disagreements, deepening your relationships and making them more
durable and meaningful in the process. It is important to follow the
structure carefully.

Step one: commit to being totally authentic in all your relationships

Being authentic means not hiding behind masks. It's about
committing to getting as real as you can in your life. When you are
in conflict, be clear about your contribution to the conflict and share
your feelings about it. To bring resolution to disagreements, it is
necessary that you do not sabotage yourself by being insincere. It
takes courage to be authentic, but by doing so you will be building
a healthy sense of self-esteem.

EXERCISE
GET REAL

Think of a situation in your life in which you are not being
real and authentic. Now ask yourself the following
questions, writing down the answers in your journal.

- Why is it that I am afraid to be authentic in this
  situation?

- What do I need to give up or let go of in order to be
  authentic in this situation?

- Who can I get feedback and support from to access my
  authenticity?

$$-\;\ell\;-$$

Arrange to meet with an anger buddy who can witness you being
your authentic self. Become that person, if only for a few minutes.
Ask your anger buddy for feedback. Now become your false self,
with your anger buddy witnessing. Ask them for feedback. Now ask
yourself which you really want to be: your authentic self or your
false self. Take steps to become that self.

Step two: identify the primary needs in any given situation

We have probably all at some time become embroiled in major
conflict over a trivial thing, such as not washing the dishes, arriving
late for an appointment or forgetting to mow the lawn, knowing that
in fact the real issue lies much deeper. It is very important to
transcend surface complexities and determine what the disagreement is actually about. When we scratch beneath the surface, we
will discover that there are many underlying issues reinforcing and
compounding frequent disputes and emotional impasses. It's these
issues that leave us feeling helpless, hopeless and despairing. This

is why identifying our primary needs and getting them met is the foundation to resolving ongoing disagreements.

We have already noted (on page 70) that conflict rises out of our primary needs not being met and that it is our responsibility to identify what these needs are and either meet them ourselves or ensure that they are met in a healthy way by someone else. In order to resolve conflict, we also need to ascertain what the primary needs are of the other person.

EXERCISE
IDENTIFYING AND MEETING PRIMARY NEEDS

Think of a conflict in your life, then ask yourself the following questions, writing the answers in your journal.

- What are my primary needs in this situation?

- How can I tell the other person what my needs are without escalating the disagreement?

- How can I identify the other person's primary needs?

- Can I suggest to them what their primary needs might be without making assumptions or escalating the disagreement?

- How can I meet my needs or get them met?

- How can I meet the other person's needs or encourage them to get them met?

$$-\;\text{\textit{4}}\;-$$

Step three: think both/and rather than either/or

There is a part in all of us that just loves to be right. If we are not right, then we must be wrong, and being wrong can often equate in our minds to 'there is something wrong with me'. It's that 'there is something wrong with me' that our ego cannot tolerate – it cannot tolerate its own imperfections. But life is not in reality about right and wrong; it's about respecting and validating diversity and difference in both ourselves and in others.

Being right fits nicely into the either/or paradigm, but when it comes to managing our anger in disagreements, we need to embody the both/and paradigm. Rather than 'us and them', we need to remember that there is only 'us'. If we focus our attention on dualities and opposites, we have already lost the battle.

EXERCISE
BOTH/AND THINKING

Think of a conflict in your life, then ask yourself the following questions, writing the answers in your journal.

- In this conflict, am I stuck in either/or thinking?
- Is the other person stuck in either/or thinking?
- Can I shift the paradigm to both/and thinking without having to give anything up?
- What might I lose by shifting the paradigm to both/and thinking?
- What might I gain by shifting the paradigm to both/and thinking?

— ⚡ —

Step four: identify workable solutions

I have heard it said that a problem is only a problem when you cannot find a solution; otherwise, it's not a problem but a creative endeavour. The process of identifying solutions is only accessible when you think outside the box. This means thinking laterally rather than linearly.

Identifying solutions also requires you to be in your adult self rather than your wounded, regressed child mode. Being in your adult gives you access to reasoning, logic, creativity and imagination. It enables you to be coherent and focused. Only by remaining in your adult can you transcend your own limitations and work to overcome conflict.

EXERCISE
IDENTIFYING SOLUTIONS

Think of a conflict in your life, then make a list of four possible solutions in your journal. Now, taking each solution in turn, consider the following:

1 Do I have more than one really workable resolution to the problem?

2 Have I considered all the possible options for resolution?

3 Is there any possible resolution that I know I cannot live with?

4 Have I eliminated that choice from the list?

5 Is there any choice that I know the other person could not live with?

6 Have I eliminated that choice from the list?

7 Having eliminated the choices that are unacceptable to either me or the other person, do I still have more than one possible solution?

8 If I have only one solution, can I identify additional possible solutions that may be acceptable?

9 Of the remaining possible solutions, are there any that will not work (i.e. where I know there is or will be an obstacle)?

10 Have I eliminated from the list those solutions that I know cannot work?

11 Do I still have more than one possible workable solution?

12 Of the possible solutions that can work, which choice fulfils most of my personal interests?

13 Would this solution be acceptable to the other person or does it need to be adjusted in some way to be made more acceptable?

14 How can the solution be adjusted, if necessary, to become acceptable to the other person?

15 If it cannot be adjusted, is there another choice that still satisfies my crucial issues but may be more readily acceptable to the other person?

16 Am I satisfied that I have completely reviewed all possible workable solutions?

17 Have I prepared alternative solutions in the event that my first choice or best solution does not resolve the problem?

18 Am I now prepared to present my first choice of solution to the other person?

19 Have I considered that the chance of a proposal being accepted often lies not in the proposal itself but in how it is presented?

20 Knowing that the presentation of the proposal is a key element in its chances of success, have I prepared my presentation in any way (for example with flowers, with a beautiful notecard, at a special occasion, after a good meal)?

21 Do I now feel complete with the conflict-solving process? If not, what else do I need to do in order for the process to feel complete?

(Adapted from *Ironing It Out*, by Charles P. Lickson)

— ⚡ —

Step five: follow the clearing process

The clearing process is a key component in resolving conflict. If possible, it is a good idea to teach this process to the people you are close to, so that should conflict arise between you, you will all be able to participate in the process fully. If you are unable to clear with the person concerned use your anger buddy.

The clearing process is discussed in greater detail on page 213. For now, all you need to know is that there are six stages in the process. Each of these represents an aspect that needs to be considered in order for the conflict to be resolved harmoniously. The stages are:

* Data (straightforward information and incontrovertible facts)
* Opinions and judgements
* Feelings
* Wants and needs
* Shadow (what you are willing to own about your own behaviour)
* The gift (what the other person has taught you through this process)

EXERCISE
THE CLEARING PROCESS

Think of a recent conflict you have had with someone. Now go through the clearing process, using the example below as a guide.

Data

'There's no petrol in my car. I have asked when you use my car to make sure you fill it up with petrol, and you have agreed to do so. Is that correct?'

Opinions and judgements

'My opinion is that you don't take my requests seriously, and you don't follow up on what you have committed to.'

Feelings

'I feel angry and hurt when you don't listen to me.'

Wants and needs

'I need you to take me seriously, listen to me and hold yourself accountable for the things you say you will do.'

Shadow

'What I am willing to own about my own behaviour is that I also make commitments to people and then don't follow through on them. There are times when I treat others with disrespect.'

The gift

'The gift for me in this situation is to realise that you don't do things to make me angry. I make myself angry because I make up that you don't care for me when I know you truly do. At different times, each of us is irresponsible and inconsiderate towards the other. Thanks for listening.'

— ⚡ —

Step six: access empathy and compassion (keep your heart open at all times)

The spiritual teacher Ram Dass has made the basic premise of all his teachings: no matter what the situation or the circumstances, always keep your heart open. Of course, if you try suggesting this to a person who is feeling angry and hurt, it is unlikely to be well received and will quite possibly add even more fuel to the fire. Consider this question: how easy is it for you to be angry with someone and still keep your heart open? I ask this question in all my anger management groups, and rarely does anyone reply that they can be angry and still keep their heart open. Occasionally, some of the imploders in the group are able to do this, as they tend to be more readily empathetic than the exploders.

Remember that preserving relationships is the goal of all conflict resolution. Our task in confrontations is to remain empathetic and compassionate, even though there may be a part of us that wants to tear the other person's throat out.

EXERCISE
KEEPING YOUR HEART OPEN

Think of a situation, real or imagined, in which you are angry with someone and are unwilling to forgive them for their behaviour. Now ask yourself the following questions, writing the answers in your journal.

- What is my resistance to keeping my heart open (being empathetic) to the other person?

- In order to open my heart to them, what do I have to give up or let go?

- Can I identify my own shadow material in relation to the other person? Can I recognise myself in their behaviour?

- Am I willing to own my own behaviour and accept that
  I am not perfect and have at times equally impacted on
  the lives of others around me in some hurtful way, even
  though it was not my intention to be hurtful?
- Can I forgive myself?

— ⚡ —

Emotional intelligence: a key to overcoming your psychological limitations

An enormous amount has been written about emotional literacy over the last 12 years. In his book *Emotional Intelligence*, Daniel Goleman suggests that it is possible for people to learn to become more emotionally intelligent.

People who read personal development books or participate in workshops often comment that it's not that they have learnt anything new but that they've been reminded of what they once knew and had forgotten. Indeed, while 'new' theories and concepts abound in the personal development field, much of what I am writing about here is intended to serve as a reminder of the power you already hold within. Emotional intelligence is something you already possess; it's just that you've forgotten how to draw upon it to help you in your day-to-day life.

So how do we lose touch with our emotional intelligence? As a result of early childhood trauma, many of us have had to shut down emotionally because of the intensity of our emotional pain. In so doing we have disengaged from our vitality. Our unconscious priority is to make sure that our primary love needs are met, and we will do whatever it takes to meet it.

We learn from an early age how to manipulate and influence our environment in order to get these needs met. We believe that we have no choice in the matter because not having our primary needs met is emotionally painful and, for a child, can sometimes even be life-threatening. In order to avoid the pain of rejection and abandonment, we repress our other needs, but the result of this is that we grow increasingly distanced from our inner wisdom. We become inauthentic, and we end up living in an emotional wasteland. Only when we experience a major crisis do many of us accept that something has to change.

From one point of view, then, an anger management problem is actually a gift in disguise – a pathway to the rediscovery of your wisdom, to reunion with your inner jewel. It offers you the means of accessing the tools you need to turn your wasteland into a Garden of Eden, reclaiming your own magnificence, potential and sacredness.

Emotional intelligence enables you to become once more a vibrant, energised human being, equipped with the capacity and the willingness to roll with life's punches, stay in the flow and face up to the responsibilities that come with being human. It gives you space to breathe by removing you from the spiral of traumatic disintegration. And if you do get caught up in this spiral, you will be able to extricate yourself.

An important aspect of controlling your anger is your willingness to digest theoretical information and putting it to use in a practical way on a daily basis. Reminding yourself that you have the potential to heal and transform yourself will encourage you to become more emotionally effective. As this happens, your true nature will become increasingly clear and accessible, and your self-esteem and confidence will increase.

The ten ingredients of emotional intelligence
There are ten central ingredients that need to be present if we are

to become emotionally intelligent. Let's take a look at them now.

1 Self-awareness

Fostering self-awareness involves acknowledging:

* What you like and dislike
* What you yearn for, i.e. your goals, hopes and dreams
* Your preferences and your prejudices
* Your cultural identity and traditional customs
* Your talents and skills
* Your shortcomings and limitations
* What's unique about you
* Your awareness of and sensitivity to both your inner and outer world
* Your relationship to your own spirituality and religious beliefs
* Your own internal resources, i.e. remembering that you are not as helpless as you may believe

2 Management of feelings

Managing feelings involves:

* Being aware of emotions – so that you do not confuse sadness with hurt, guilt with shame, and so on
* Building an emotional vocabulary
* Understanding the difference between a feeling and a thought, a feeling and an action, a feeling and behaviour, a feeling and a sensation
* Accurately reading 'feeling cues' from others and being able to respond appropriately, for example by using body language
* Understanding what activates feelings
* Learning to communicate constructively and to contain and control your feelings

3 Decision-making

Decision-making involves:

* Making meaningful, mature and firm decisions
* Learning the logical steps to making effective decisions
* Applying logic and structured thinking to the issues you encounter in life

4 Stress management

Stress management involves:

* Understanding how stress comes about and how it affects you physically and emotionally
* Learning and making use of effective stress management techniques, such as exercise, healthy eating, meditation, guided visualisation, relaxation methods, energy and time-management, and challenging toxic thinking and negative core beliefs

5 Embracing personal responsibility

Embracing personal responsibility involves:

* Developing healthy personal boundaries
* Being clear about saying yes and no
* Having a mature awareness of your intentions, actions and decisions and the impact of their consequences
* Recognising that everything you think, feel and do is motivated by choices that you make, whether these choices are conscious or unconscious
* Taking responsibility for the choices you make whether conscious or unconscious

6 Healthy self concept

Building a healthy self-concept involves:

* Knowing that you are more than your mind, body and feelings
* Having healthy self-esteem and being able to meet your own primary needs in a mature way
* Recognising and accepting your limitations
* Recognising your own potential
* Challenging your own negative core self-beliefs
* Celebrating your own talents and abilities – and those of others

7 Empathy

Being empathetic involves:

* Keeping your heart open to others by seeing the world through their eyes
* Forming a caring and benevolent relationship with the world around you

8 Communication skills

Having good communication skillls involves:

* Learning and practising how to communicate effectively
* Using 'I' statements instead of shaming, blaming, judging or criticising others
* Learning active listening skills

9 Understanding the function of groups and their dynamics

Understanding the function of groups and their dynamics involves:

* Recognising that groups are similar to family systems

* Becoming self-reflective and aware of your own internal processes in a group environment

* Observing your behaviour and role in the group as well as that of others
* Cooperating with other group members
* Being interdependent rather than co-dependent or counter-dependent. (Co-dependent means being overly concerned about the other person rather than exploring and noticing what's going on for you and dealing with it. Counter-dependent means believing that in order to survive in the world you need to do everything yourself, never reaching out for support because people will always fail you.)
* Recognising when to follow and when to lead

10 Conflict resolution

The ability to resolve conflict involves:

* Understanding that conflict is healthy and can be very productive
* Learning how to fight fairly with others
* Learning and practising a variety of conflict resolution strategies
* Understanding the difference between compromise and win/win
* Learning how to achieve a win/win situation
* Developing empathetic negotiating skills
* Developing problem-solving techniques
* Remembering that healthy conflict can lead to intimacy

The clearing process

Every time you feel angry with another person, you either express your anger – which may, if you are not mindful in your approach, trigger a negative reaction in them – or you don't express your anger, in which case it builds inside you until eventually you explode. You are in conflict with that person and will remain so until you can resolve matters with them. If no resolution takes place, you will remain resentful or hostile, which helps no one and only serves to keep your anger alive

There is a way of expressing anger that is clean, healing and empowering for both ourselves and others. It is known as the clearing process. It enables you to confront another person in even the most challenging situation without it becoming a major drama. There are two versions of the clearing process, A and B. Both are simple yet powerful. All they require is that we express ourselves as cleanly and respectfully as possible. Try both versions at different times to find the one that is most comfortable for you, and then use it in situations of conflict. It is a good idea to practise the clearing process a few times with an anger buddy before using it for real. This will give you an opportunity to explore your own shadow material.

It is important not to enter into the clearing process while you are fuming or in the grip of regression. In this situation, it is much better to use the eight golden rules of anger management, which we will be exploring in Chapter Seven.

Before entering into the clearing process with another person, there are several things to consider:

* Make sure you are certain of the facts relating to the conflict
* Be aware that this is your work, not theirs
* Be clear that the other person does not need to justify their behaviour to you
* Make sure the other person is aware that all you need them to do is listen to you
* If you wish, you can offer the other person the opportunity

to give you feedback at the end of the clearing process

* Make sure you have allowed yourself enough time to do the clearing – check with the other person that they have enough time available. The process should not take more than 15 minutes

* Do not be attached to an outcome; sometimes the process will not go the way you want it to

* Part of the clearing process involves owning your part of your shadow; be aware that there will not always be a shadow present for you. This is OK

* Be careful not to confuse judgements and feelings with data (facts)

Clearing process A

* Ask the other person if they have 15 minutes to do the clearing process with you
  For example: 'I need to discuss an issue with you. Do you have about 15 minutes to clear this issue up?'

* Explain to the other person that you want them to just listen, and if you would like feedback at the end of the process, ask for that too
  For example: 'I just need you to listen to me and not interrupt me. At the end of the process I would appreciate feedback, thanks'

* **Data** (straightforward information and incontrovertible facts): share the facts concerning the situation.
  For example: 'We agreed we would meet, and you did not turn up'

* **Opinions and judgements**: give your opinion of the other person
  For example: 'Because you didn't turn up, I think you are

unfeeling and uncaring. In my opinion, you only think about
yourself.'

* **Feelings**: Identify what you feel in the moment. It is
  important to be clear and concise about how you feel.
  For example: 'I feel angry with you.'
* **Wants and needs**: state clearly what you want or need
  from the other person in the future (bearing in mind that
  you may not get it).
  For example: 'What I want from you is that you to stick to the
  commitments you make and call me if you're running late.'
* **Shadow:** state what you are willing to own about your own
  shadow (or behaviour).
  For example: 'What I am willing to own about my own
  behaviour is that … yes, sometimes I also arrive late for
  appointments.'
* **The gift:** this is the overall learning that you have gained
  from following this process. It is about cultivating
  awareness of the benefits of doing a clearing with the other
  person. (The key benefit is enabling us to express our
  anger towards the other person while at the same time
  honouring them and developing a healthy understanding of
  ourselves.)
  For example: 'The gift in doing this process with you is that
  I now realise how easy it is to project my issues onto you,
  without seeing that it is really all about my own fear, anger
  and hurt.'
* If you wish, ask the other person for feedback (but
  remember that the clearing is about you rather than the
  other person).
  For example: 'Is there any feedback you would like to give
  me?'

Clearing process B

If the person you are clearing with is very defensive or insecure, they may not be open to hearing the judgements that you are required to share in clearing process A and may become reactive. In this case, clearing process B may be more effective. Clearing process B is also useful if you are seeking to understand the historical source of unprocessed trauma. You should always start your sentences with the words given in bold at the start of each bullet point – 'I feel', 'Because, 'When' and so on.

* **'I feel …':** Express your feelings with regard to this situation.

  For example: 'I feel angry with you.'

* **'Because …':** Explain why you feel this way.

  For example: 'Because I have asked you several times already to take out the rubbish and you still haven't done it.'

* **'When …':** This question locates the regressive component in your anger. You are looking for the instance in the past that has really triggered your anger.

  For example: 'When I was a child, my father and mother had arguments about this, I felt really scared and confused.'

* **'What I want is …'** Explain what you want of the other person (bearing in mind that they may not give it to you).

  For example: 'What I want is for you to do what you have agreed to do without me having to ask you again and again.'

* **'What I am willing to own about my own behaviour is** …' This is where you own your own shadow material.

  For example: 'What I am willing to own about my own behaviour is that often I do not follow through on the commitments that I make.'

When I teach the clearing process, I often get reactions such as, 'I could never say that to my boss – he would fire me!', or 'You must be joking! This will never work with my wife. It will just make things worse.' My response is always, 'Try it and see.' People are generally amazed at how well the process works. When we own up to our own shadow projections, the other person understands that our anger is not really about them at all, but is about us, and they are able to hear what we need to say without reacting negatively.

EXERCISE
CLEARING UNFINISHED
BUSINESS

Think of someone with whom you have unfinished business.

•

Contact this person and use the clearing process (either A or B, depending on which seems most appropriate) to share with them what you could have said at the time.

•

Reflect on this experience in your journal.

— ⚡ —

CHAPTER 7

The Eight Golden Rules of Anger Management

If you only use one technique outlined in this book, make it the eight golden rules of anger management. These rules should be etched into your memory. They will enable you to avoid going into angry meltdown, enabling you to deal with your own and other people's anger safely. With practice, they will become the cornerstone of a new set of healthy habits for managing your anger appropriately.

There are hundreds of theoretical models for managing and containing anger, each of which has its merits, but this one, founded on aggression prevention training is for me far and away the most effective, because it doesn't rely on you remembering, in the heat of the moment, a whole range of coping strategies. All you have to remember are eight simple rules. These rules have been synthesised from a range of different theories, and each one is common-sense, practical and simple to apply in the heat of the moment. They can be used individually or all together, depending on the situation.

I suggest you make your own abbreviated version of the golden rules, listing each one in turn. You can take photocopies of this, laminate them and keep them in your car, near the fridge, in your bathroom, on your desk ... so that there will always be a copy visible and to hand if you feel yourself beginning to become angry. Eventually, you should memorise the rules. The more you practise them, the easier they become to remember and put into action. Learning the eight golden rules has saved me in many situations and will continue to support me for the rest of my life.

Rule 1: Back off, stop, think, take a look at the big picture

Old woman / young woman illusion

The optical illusion above illustrates that there are many different ways of looking at a single situation. In order to see the big picture, we need to back off and take time to think.

In Ireland there is a wonderful saying: 'There are three truths: my truth, your truth and the truth.' When we stop and look at the big picture, we are able to see things from other people's perspectives, which are often completely different from our own. The inability to step back in this way almost guarantees that we will carry a heavy weight of anger with us through life. When we are unable to see things through other people's eyes, we tend to experience others as threatening – and when we feel threatened, the fight, flight or freeze mechanism is activated, beginning the meltdown into anger.

I like to see 'back off' as an acronym. It goes like this:

B Breathe

A Adapt

C Calm down – and remain that way

K Keep cool

O Organise your thoughts

F Feel your feelings

F Forgive yourself and the other person

Often we react before we have taken the time to see what is really happening in a given situation. We jump to conclusions, failing to see the big picture and therefore to understand the situation for what it is. As a result we may speak hurtful words that can never be taken back and that cause a great deal of damage.

One of the biggest problems of angry people is that they don't think about the consequences of their actions until it's too late. This is why the first golden rule of anger management is so important. Just think about it: the first words are '*back off, stop*'. When we stop there is the possibility for something different from rage to occur. By stopping we give ourselves time – time in which to determine the appropriate response to the situation and implement it.

We tend to want to deal with situations while we are still in a hyper-aroused emotional state. This rule of anger management makes sure you stop, step back and take time out before acting in the heat of the moment – and quite probably regretting it later.

When you take time out, you are able to consider:

* How you feel
* The potential consequences of your actions, behaviour and thoughts
* Whether you are regressed and behaving like an infant
* What other choices are available to you
* What your needs are in this situation
* What the other person's needs may be in this situation
* Whether you are over-reacting and being melodramatic
* What shadows are being triggered in you and why
* What shadows may be being triggered for the other person and why
* Whether you are taking what the other person is doing and saying personally
* How you could resolve the conflict without having to go into battle

When we back off and give ourselves breathing space, we are using voluntary time management. If we do not do this of our own free will, we may find ourselves in a position where we have no choice in the matter. When, for example, we have flown into a rage, beaten someone up and are now sitting in a police cell waiting for a solicitor to bail us out, we are being compelled (by another) to think about the consequences of our actions.

If we can develop the degree of self-discipline required to back off in this way, we have a good chance of increasing our level of self-awareness. I like to think of 'aware' as an acronym:

A Acknowledge and accept that there is a problem

W Wait without reacting, noticing whether you are regressing

A Anchor yourself in order to begin calming yourself down

R Respond appropriately, making an 'I' statement: ('I feel …')

E Empathise – come from the heart

Let's have a look at this in more detail.

Acknowledge and accept that there is a problem

Many people I have worked with on anger management issues say that initially they are often not even aware that they are angry; it takes a while before they are able to recognise what they are feeling. Some say that they are also frequently unaware when other people are in conflict with them.

Anger management is about increasing our sensitivity to the presence of conflict. Once we are able to recognise that we are feeling angry, we can acknowledge it to ourselves and to others. We can also affirm to ourselves that it's OK to feel angry and that anger is healthy as long as it is expressed in appropriate ways. We can also also speak to others in a clear and open way about the conflict. Suitable approaches might be:

* 'I can see we're not getting on. Do you want to talk about it, because I would like to when you're ready?'
* 'I'm aware that we have a few issues we need to deal with. Can we take time to talk about them, either now or later?'

Another alternative would be to use clearing process A (see page 215).

Wait without reacting, noticing whether you are regressing

I personally find waiting patiently a difficult thing to do. However, it is the only practical course of action in a conflict situation. If the other person is not ready to deal with the issue at stake, there is no point in going in there in a gung-ho manner. This approach will only backfire. In this situation, we need to learn how to sit in the discomfort of our own feelings and wait, without reacting to the other person.

Anchor yourself in order to begin calming yourself down

Anchoring yourself means grounding yourself and stabilising your body sensations so that you don't lose the plot. There are various techniques for doing this, but the simplest and most effective method is to focus on your breath, inhaling and exhaling deeply until the adrenaline rushing through your body eventually slows. Other useful strategies include:

* Counting backwards from 21 to 1
* Breathing in for seven seconds out for eleven seconds (7/11 breathing)
* Walking away from the incident until such time as you are able to deal with it in a mature and healthy manner
* Talking yourself into a state of calm by telling yourself aloud, 'Cool it ... Back off, now.'
* Relaxing any clenched muscles
* Going to a special relaxing place in your mind (for example imagining yourself on a beach in the sun)
* Ignoring anger triggers and mindgames
* Not taking anything personally
* Recognising that you are having expectations of someone or something and letting them go

* Distracting yourself by doing something different
* Empathising with the other person's situation
* Practising tolerance
* Smiling or laughing
* Thinking positive
* Telling yourself that everything will calm down soon

Respond appropriately, making an 'I' statement

When you open your mouth, make sure that whatever comes out is not designed to hurt the other person emotionally. Remember that if you express aggression and hostility, you give your power away. If you are able to say in the moment, 'I feel angry when you …' this can actually be transformative and will definitely help to calm the situation down. Another strategy is to do clearing process B (see page 217). Choose your time with care, however – good timing can make for a much less explosive situation.

Empathise – come from the heart

When we are angry, wrapped up in our own bewildering feelings, it is very difficult to be empathetic towards the other person – even to consider them as another individual. The way out of this situation is to allow ourselves to experience and express the whole range of our feelings. If we can allow ourselves to reveal our inner world and show our vulnerability, we will immediately give the other person permission to do the same. Speaking from the heart breaks through every game – and it is what we all yearn for.

Part of having empathy is about recognising that what you are sharing may be difficult for the other person to hear. They will need time to digest, absorb and come to terms with it. Giving them the time and space to do this shows them that you care. Having empathy is about recognising that we all struggle to various degrees. Understanding this is the key to our humanity. It leaves us open to possibility, not limited by ideas about how things should or shouldn't be.

Having empathy for ourselves is as important as having empathy for others, but if we are shame-bound it may be very difficult for us to do this. Indeed, empathising with others may be easier than recognising that we ourselves are struggling, or are in pain in situations of conflict. Bear in mind that we need to keep our heart open to ourselves as well as to others.

Rule 2: It's OK to have a different opinion

Opinions are not facts, and trying to impose them on others is aggressive and abusive. Our opinions are our own subjective realities based on our own particular life experiences, belief system, values and judgements. They are not universal truths and they are neither right nor wrong.

When we are angry, we often have rigid values, ideas and beliefs about how we think others should be, how we should be and how life should be. We may come across as opinionated, critical, judgemental, egocentric and narcissistic. We experience life mostly in black and white, positive and negative, right and wrong, good and bad, should and shouldn't. We tend to think linearly (either/or thinking) rather than laterally (both/and thinking). Lateral thinking is thinking outside of the box. It allows us to be flexible, open to difference and diversity, and in this context our relationship with ourselves and with others blossoms. Lateral thinking enhances our ability to empathise.

The key to releasing ourselves into this kind of thinking is to remember that opinions are only that. If a person says something about you that you are certain is not true, remember it is only their opinion and probably says more about them than about you. It is very possible that they are projecting their shadows onto you.

If you are struggling with this second golden rule, try remembering the following statements when you are in the heat of conflict:

* I don't have to defend my point of view and win the argument
* I don't have to let someone else's opinion irritate me
* Our differences of opinion do not need to affect our relationship
* We can agree to disagree
* Opinions are not facts

Boundaries

Part of rule two is about establishing healthy boundaries. We have a responsibility to ourselves to be clear about our boundaries. If our boundaries are not clear, we will be in a constant state of confusion and turmoil.

The me/you/us rule

A simple way to establish boundaries in a heated situation is to apply the me/you/us rule. Ask yourself:

* Is this about me?
* Is this about you (the other person)?
* Is this about us?

If it is about you, you need to accept and take responsibility for your actions and feelings.

If it is about the other person, you do not have to take what they are saying personally or be emotionally affected by it or them.

If it is about us, there is a problem that you need to resolve together. If this is to be done respectfully, it may need to happen after some time out for both parties to think, calm down and make use of their support networks.

Rule 3: Listen actively

Listening is one of the crucial requirements in anger management.
If you are not listening, you are not learning. You are not taking in
accurate information that enables you to make sense of the situation.

Listening is an art. We all know how difficult it is to listen to
someone when we feel angry with them – particularly when our
primal instincts have been activated and our body is preparing for
fight or flight. When we're in this state we tend to hear what is said
through a filter of fear or anger, with the result that we make up
what the person is saying rather than hearing what is actually said.
The more regressed we become, the more difficult it is to hear the
other person accurately and remain empathetic and open-minded
– and if the other person senses that we are not listening, they will
feel unheard, and this may become a trigger for their own anger.

So what are the qualities of a good listener. Here are the key ones:

* Good listeners concentrate
* Good listeners are emotionally mature
* Good listeners have good powers of recall (good memory)
* Good listeners are open-minded
* Good listeners make few mistakes
* Good listeners are popular
* Good listeners are successful
* Good listeners are wise
* Good listeners are slow to anger

EXERCISE
DO YOU HAVE THE QUALITIES OF A GOOD LISTENER?

Read the following statements, circling 'Yes' for those that apply to you and 'No' for those that you need to work on.

1	I have good powers of concentration.	Yes	No
2	I am emotionally mature.	Yes	No
3	I have a good memory.	Yes	No
4	I am open-minded.	Yes	No
5	I make few mistakes.	Yes	No
6	I am popular.	Yes	No
7	I am wise.	Yes	No
8	I am slow to anger.	Yes	No

Make a note in your journal of the statements that you circled 'No' for. These are the qualities you need to begin the process of developing.

— ⚡ —

Listen with LOVE

Try this simple tool for listening. It comes wrapped in the memorable acronym, LOVE.

L Learn

Be open to learning. As long as you are speaking, you are not learning. Be attentive and focused on what the other person is saying. Make sure you understand the facts, and stick to them!

O Observe

Observe the other person's tone of voice, body language and emotions. Eighty-five per cent of all communication is non-verbal.

V Verify

Ask questions in order to clarify your understanding.

Paraphrase what you have heard in order to check that it is correct. For example, 'What I understand you are saying is … Am I right?'

E Empathise

Acknowledge how and why the other person feels what they feel. An ability to be open-hearted towards them will go a long way towards helping you to control your anger.

Empathy versus sympathy

At this point, I'd like to take some time to make the distinction between empathy and sympathy. It's easy to get the two confused, but they have entirely different meanings.

Sympathy is the feeling (or the expression of the feeling) of pity for someone else's pain or distress. Sympathy implies feeling sorry for the other person, which will generally lead them to feel patronised. None of us wants other people to feel sorry for us. Sympathy often involves an over-identification with the sufferer and a desire to take their pain away. This is understandable, but in order to take responsibility for ourselves it is crucial that we are allowed to feel our own pain and our own feelings, even when they seem overwhelming. This process enables us to become familiar with our own emotional landscape. We cannot do this if our experiences are hijacked or 'fixed' by another person.

Empathy, on the other hand, is about acknowledging the experiences and feelings of others without intruding our need to fix them or make them feel OK about themselves. This allows the other person space to deal with their own pain and distress.

In his book, *The Essential Difference*, Simon Baron-Cohen describes empathy as the natural, spontaneous ability to tune in to another person's thoughts and feelings, whatever they might be.

According to Baron-Cohen,

It is not about just reacting to a small number of emotions and feelings in others, such as pain or sadness; it is about reading the emotional atmosphere between people. It is about effortlessly putting yourself into another's shoes, sensitively negotiating an interaction with another person so as not to hurt or offend them in any way, caring about another's feelings. The ability to identify with and understand another person's feelings or difficulties.

He goes on to say:

Empathy is a defining feature of human relationships. For example, empathy stops you doing things that would hurt another person's feelings. Empathy makes you bite your lip, rather than say something that may offend or make them feel hurt or rejected. Empathy also stops you inflicting physical pain on a person or animal. You may feel angry toward your dog for barking, but you don't hit him because you know he would suffer. Empathy helps you tune in to someone else's world; you have to set your own world aside – your perceptions, knowledge, assumptions or feelings. Empathy drives you to care for, or offer comfort to, another person, even if they are unrelated to you and you stand to gain nothing in return.

Most of us find it fairly easy to experience empathy towards others when we are in a state of calm; when we are angry, however, the exact opposite tends to occur. We demonise the other person, turning them into the enemy. Being angry and keeping our heart open is certainly a challenging task.

The more we learn to control our anger, the more space we create in our life for empathy. And, ultimately, it is our ability to access empathy that will transform our relationship with anger. Through empathy we develop the ability to forgive ourselves for making mistakes, getting things wrong and acting out dysfunctionally.

Techniques for good listening

Being a good listener requires that you use certain techniques. These techniques might sound basic, but remember, applying them is much more challenging when you are feeling overwhelmed and distressed. The key techniques are:

* Stop talking and listen
* Hear what is being said rather what you want to hear
* Resist the temptation to interrupt (interrupting stops the flow)
* Don't fidget
* Show you are listening and look interested and empathetic.
* Hold on to a desire to learn the facts
* Contain and control outbursts of feeling
* Don't argue or criticise (it's not about winning or losing; it's about listening)
* When the speaker pauses, ask questions to clarify the situation (this shows you are interested and helps you understand the other person)
* Keep an open mind
* Remain non-judgemental
* Listen for incongruencies – but do not challenge them.
* Keep your heart open
* Face the speaker and look into their eyes
* Remain relaxed and attentive
* Keep an open mind
* Use body language (for example nodding) or some other form of acknowledgement (for example saying 'uh huh' to show you are listening

EXERCISE
HOW GOOD A LISTENER ARE YOU?

Using the above list for guidance, write down in your journal your three strongest qualities as a listener?

•

Now list your three weakest qualities as a listener.

•

Write down three things that you can do to become a better listener.

— ⚡ —

Listening to someone who is angry

When a person is angry, the last thing you want to do is to fuel the already raging fire. The best approach is to let them know you are listening, and keep listening until such time as they naturally begin to calm down. It is important that you do everything in your power not to regress, because if this happens, the situation is likely to turn into an all-out war. Use the FLOW process (see page 52) and the AWARE process (see pages 223) to help you. Here are some pointers for listening without escalating the situation:

* Listen to the person's point of view and try to put yourself in their shoes – it helps to access empathy towards them.

* Contain your need to become defensive – if you become defensive, you will hear nothing that is being said. (The most effective way to avoid becoming defensive is to remind yourself not to take anything personally (see page 52).

* However illogical the other person may sound, this is what they are thinking and experiencing – try to respect it. If you

feel your anger rising, remind yourself that they are probably regressed and may be trying to regress you.

* When a person is angry, they really believe they are in the right; therefore this is *not* a good time to challenge them in any way.
* Encourage the person to share the facts rather than escalate their own anger.
* Although it's important to let the person vent their feelings, if they become abusive remind them in a neutral way that this is unacceptable.
* Encourage the person to wait until they have calmed down before attempting to deal with any problems – i.e. 'Let's talk about this when we're both feeling a bit calmer.'
* Acknowledge that you can accept that this is what they feel without having to agree with it.
* Apply the me/you/us rule (see page 227).

Don't say/do say

Let's take a look at constructive phrasing to use when addressing a person who is feeling angry.

Don't say	Do say
'I know just how you must feel!' (This can come across as patronising)	'It sounds like you are having a challenging time. This must be the last straw for you.'
'Calm down or I won't speak to you!'	'I can hear how angry and upset you are. Take as much time as you need to express it.'
'Why don't you take a deep	'It's much healthier to let

breath and relax?'

'Do you think you're the only
person with problems?!'

'Don't be so silly!'

your anger out than keep it
in.'

'Take as much time as you
need to tell me what's
going on for you.'

'It does sound as if you
have a good point.'

Do men and women listen differently?

This is an age-old question that has been much discussed. In her
book, *You Just Don't Understand*, Deborah Tannen suggests that
there is a difference in how men and women listen. According to
Tannen, women tend to engage in 'rapport talk' – in other words,
they often focus their talk around making connections and maintaining relationships. When they are in reactive mode, their rapport
talk shifts to language designed to soothe, reassure or rescue.

Men, on the other hand, engage in 'report talk', which is geared
to providing information and solving problems. In reactive mode this
will often take the form of trying to 'fix' the situation, asking
questions or offering solutions.

And finally ...

Clearly, listening is a huge subject. Arguably, much of the pain in
the world today is caused by our inability to listen to each other.
Here are a few points to remember:

* We all like to be right; it's part of the human condition
* We read one another's body language before we hear what
  each other has to say
* When we are busy trying to figure out how to make our own

issues known, most of us are poor listeners
* When we stop and listen, we hear things we have never heard before
* When we are trying to win an argument, we are often not interested in what the other person is saying
* No one is a winner when it comes to conflict

Rule 4: Use your emotional support network (anger buddies)

We have discussed support networks briefly on pages 7–8. Your support network is a group of people that you can call on when you need to talk so that your anger doesn't get out of control. They may be visited, phoned, texted or emailed. They are the people who will tell you what you *need* to hear rather than what you *want* to hear.

It is essential to have a support network if you want to befriend your anger and build healthy relationships in your life. After all, when you're faced with a lifetime of destructive and self-sabotaging habits, as well as 770 million years' worth of pre-programmed sub-conscious responses, you need all the help you can get. When you're going into meltdown, it helps to know that there are people in your life who represent an anchor to sanity.

One of the major reasons why people who go on struggling with their anger is that they do not have enough emotional support to enable them to get to grips with this problem. When we are angry, we tend to frighten people away, thus becoming isolated and depressed – two more activators for anger. However, it is possible to develop a support network for yourself. (For more on how to do this, see page 238.)

I use the following acronym to explain why support is absolutely essential.

S Safety

There is safety in numbers . You can use people in your support network as a sounding board for problems that arise in your life around your anger.

U Uncovering

The people in your support network can help you to uncover deeper issues by giving you more perspective on what's really going on for you.

P Precautions

Your anger buddies can remind you of all the precautions you need to take in order to beat your anger: observing the eight golden rules, following the clearing process, using the detour method, becoming aware of your shadow projections, identifying your primary needs, holding to the commitment you have made to beat your anger once and for all.

P Perceptions

The great thing about anger buddies is that they can challenge your perceptions of yourself and others, so helping you to gain clarity. They can also challenge you to look at your shadows and give you an opportunity to reflect on and understand your own agenda in heated situations.

O Opportunities

Your support network can help you to identify the different opportunities available to us for changing and accepting ourselves. Anger can become the gift of transforming our lives if we can allow ourselves to read its message and learn how to express anger in a clean and healthy way once and for all.

R Responding maturely

When you open your mouth, it's important that what emerges from it are healing words. By responding with empathy and kindness rather than hostility and aggression, you pave the way for intimacy and connection rather than combat.

T Trust

Trust in yourself and in others. People are not out to get you. If
you can befriend your own shadow, you will find that your trust
in yourself and in others naturally increases. When you can
trust yourself to control your anger, your health will improve,
your stress levels will fall and your ability to enjoy life will be
enhanced.

Qualities to look for in an anger buddy

Your anger buddies need to be:

* Honest
* Reliable
* Accountable
* Possessed of integrity
* Trustworthy
* Authentic
* Responsibile

How to develop a support network

Make a list of eight people you can ask for support. It is important
to consider that anger issues do not always occur between 9am and
5pm, so you should choose individuals who will understand if you
ring them at 3am. For this reason it can be useful to recruit anger
buddies overseas, as the time difference means you can ring them
in the small hours without getting them out of bed.

For ideas of people you might consider asking for support, look
back at page 8 of Useful Tools. Another good way to recruit anger
buddies is to join an anger management group. On my ten-week
anger management courses there are between 12 and 20 participants. Within the first two weeks a bond naturally begins to emerge
among group members, because – often for the first time in their
lives – they feel that they are not alone and recognise that there are

others out there in the same boat. Participants quickly begin to turn to one another for emotional support and encouragement, and because the programme teaches them how to listen, they are able to support one another empathically.

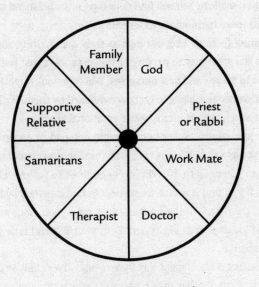

Example of support network

Use your emotional support network to make your anger management programme work for you.

Rule 5: Keep an anger management journal

We talked about keeping an anger management journal in the Useful Tools section (see page 8), and you have also been using your journal to complete many of the exercises in this book. Journalling about your experiences of conflict is also a powerful way of de-escalating anger and bringing it into proportion. It is a space where you can express your feelings safely.

Defining how we feel is important. Sometimes we wake up happy, sometimes grumpy and sometimes we wake up unsure of how we feel. But we can choose how we will experience each day and, if necessary, change our attitude accordingly. This takes practice, but it's worth the effort. You will find your days more balanced and relationships more harmonious as a result.

Avoiding feelings keeps things as they are. Writing about our feelings is a great way to explore them – a process that is essential if we are to accept and heal ourselves. When we look directly at our feelings, we are less likely to feel overwhelmed by them. We learn to handle them and thus increase our emotional literacy.

Your journal can be kept on a simple notepad or even on tape. You don't have to write in it every day; rather, you should use it as and when you need to. Nor do you need to write pages – although you can if you find it useful. Some people find it beneficial to write down all the details of their experiences with anger. Your journal is a way of logging what is happening in your life and how you are feeling about it.

Journalling is also a great way to remember the details of an event or series of events that may have made you angry and to resolve your problems in a mature way. After a while, your journal may begin to reveal patterns in your feelings and how you react, which in turn will help you to focus on and address these issues.

Of course, you can write about your experiences with anger in any way that works for you, but if you are wondering how to begin, here are some ideas:

* Describe the event that triggered your anger.
* Describe the full range of feelings you experienced. Writing about your feelings is a good way to make sense of them, and you will feel better after discharging them in a way that hurts no one.

* Write about the positive feelings as well as the negative ones. Record what you feel good about.
* Explore ways in which you could have reacted differently – either to deal with the situation more positively or, on the other hand, to deescalate it into even more conflict!

The following are questions you might find it useful to ask yourself in your anger journal. You may want to photocopy them and paste them in the front of your journal. This will support you when journalling.

* Am I applying all the eight golden rules of anger management?
* Am I acknowledging and accepting responsibility for my behaviour?
* Am I defending, justifying or making excuses for my behaviour?
* Can I acknowledge my own shortcomings and forgive myself?
* Can I be empathetic and keep my heart open to others?
* Am I dealing with issues as and when they arise?
* Am I in the here and now or in the past or future?
* Am I being clear about my personal boundaries?
* Am I being respectful of other people's boundaries?
* Am I aware of needs that are not being met?
* Can I meet them myself?
* What shadows am I not owning for myself?
* Am I using defence mechanisms, such as denial?
* Am I beating myself up because I have acted out in anger?
* Am I being passive-aggressive?
* How did I wake up this morning? Tired, confused, scared, overwhelmed ...?

✳ When did I last speak to someone in my support network?

One of the primary purposes of an anger management journal is to provide a means of externalising your anger. As you look back over the entries you can begin to observe:

✳ Patterns that you had not been aware of
✳ Reccurring triggers
✳ The choices you make in dealing with issues
✳ Unfamiliar feelings becoming accessible to you

Rule 6: Don't take things personally

John Lee suggests that, 'Almost all criticisms are a projection.' And it is not just criticisms that are projected; it is also fantasies and dreams. As long as we accept the criticisms, opinions, behaviours and actions of others as being to do with us, we are at their mercy. When you can reject them, we release ourselves from a great deal of needless pain and suffering! Of course, achieving this kind of detachment is a very difficult task, but it does get easier with practice.

I used to take everything personally. A person could shrug a shoulder or roll an eyeball, or even slightly flick their hands, and immediately it was all about me. If you are a person who is shame-bound, you probably take everything personally as well. And when you take things personally, your anger is triggered and you become both defensive and aggressive. By recognising that everything is not about me, gradually I was able to defuse the explosions of anger in my body. Finally, I came to realise that every time I took something personally, I was actually rejecting and abandoning myself.

Many of us have the habit of using information we have learned about ourselves against ourselves. There are various psychological terms for this behaviour, including negative core beliefs, private logic, and mistaken notions and beliefs. No matter what the terminology, the theory is that when we were younger – perhaps very young – we misinterpreted other people's behaviour towards us and then used the 'information' we had gained against ourselves, as a way of protecting us from our own repressed aggression and hostility. We believed that if we spoke what we really felt, others would reject or abandon us.

In reality, as we have already mentioned, the only person who can reject or abandon us is ourselves. No one else can do this to us. One way to reject or abandon ourselves is to take what other people say and do personally, even when it's not really about us. The best way to deal with this is to use the me/you/us technique described on page 227.

I am aware that at this point some readers may be chomping at the bit and saying, 'Well, it *is* personal. How can it not be personal when people say negative things about me?' My response is this: you have a choice whether to take it personally or not. The moment you take it personally, you stimulate negative core beliefs about yourself. Why would you want to do this to yourself? See if you can hear someone's criticisms without internally destroying yourself.

Negative core beliefs

Our core beliefs usually relate to some condition that we consider critical for our happiness, for example:

* Being lovable
* Being in control
* Being powerful
* Being special
* Being entitled

When these core beliefs are challenged by statements that others make, a distorted thought process is automatically activated in our brain. This is a negative core belief. For example:

* I'm unlovable
* I'm stupid
* My opinion does not count
* I am not respected
* No one likes me, however hard I try
* I am a failure
* I am useless
* I'm ugly
* I'm a bad person

Does it feel familiar? If you take time to reflect on whether these negative core beliefs are actually true, you will probably find that they are not. They are simply based on what you have made up about yourself to reinforce your negative self-sabotaging stories. These stories just support your self-fulfilling prophecies about what a bad, unworthy person you are.

EXERCISE
IDENTIFYING NEGATIVE
CORE BELIEFS

This exercise will help you to identify what you take personally, and what your negative core beliefs are.

In your journal, make a list of five things that you take personally. Then list alongside them the core belief (or self-rejecting statement) that lies beneath them. For example:

I take it personally when others say:	My negative core belief is:

You're useless!	I am of no value to anyone.
You're old fashioned.	I've got nothing to offer.
You're talking rubbish.	I'm stupid.
You never listen to me.	I am uncaring.
You're putting words into my mouth.	I am not worthy of your respect.

$$-\,\frac{1}{2}\,-$$

Challenging negative core beliefs

John Bradshaw, in his book *The Shame that Binds You*, suggests that in the course of our life we hear about 54,000 hours of negative self-messaging – in other words, two hours a day over a lifespan of 80 years. That's six whole years assuming that we sleep for eight hours each night. In order to beat your anger once and for all, you need to turn these negative messages around by challenging the way your thinking is structured. You can do this by replacing negative core beliefs with affirmations. For example:

Negative core belief	Affirmation
You're useless!	I am a valuable person.
You're old fashioned.	I am a creative being.
You're talking rubbish.	I am an original thinker.
You never listen to me.	I listen carefully.
You're putting words into my mouth.	My thoughts and opinions are important.

EXERCISE
CHALLENGING NEGATIVE
CORE BELIEFS

Arrange to meet with an anger buddy. With the help of
your buddy, identify something you have recently taken
personally. To help you to identify your distorted thought
about this, your anger buddy repeatedly asks the following
questions (choosing whichever seems most appropriate):

- What does this mean?
- Why is that so bad?

Your anger buddy should continue asking until you arrive at
the negative core belief beneath your reaction. For example:

You: I took it personally that he thought my opinion was
insignificant.

Anger buddy: What does this mean?

You: Maybe what I am saying *is* insignificant.

Anger buddy: What does this mean?

You: I am not intelligent!

Anger buddy: What does this mean?

You: I am not respected.

Anger buddy: Why is that so bad?

You: I am unlovable.

Anger buddy: What does this mean?

You: I cannot be happy without his love. (NEGATIVE CORE
BELIEF)

Once you have discovered your negative core belief, your
anger buddy should prompt you to create an affirmation
that counters it. Take your time to do this. For example:

Anger buddy: What affirmation can you create for yourself
to counter this negative core belief?

You: I value myself!

— ϟ —

Rule 7: Let go of expectations

According to John Lee, 'Expectations are unrealized resentments
waiting to happen!' But letting go of expectations – expectations of
how life, other people or your own situation 'should' be – is definitely
one of the most difficult emotional tasks. Have you noticed that
when your anger is triggered, it is always because of an expectation
you have of yourself or someone else – that a particular thing 'should'
have been said, that a person 'should' have behaved in a certain way,
that you 'should' have completed, done more, said less ... or
whatever. Personally, I notice that when I have an angry outburst it
is usually because I feel let down or disappointed by someone else's
actions or inaction.

When we set very high expectations of ourselves and others, our
anger is usually not very far from the surface as a result. The
'shoulds' begin to build up in our head. In my own case, I often
compound the situation by telling myself I 'should not' be putting
myself under this kind of pressure. Then I beat myself up because
I am not meeting the expectation I have placed on myself that I will
take care of myself. This is a form of striving to be perfect, and, of
course, it is an impossible order that only increases my resentments,
frustrations and anger.

Why do we have expectations and why do we impose them on others?

In my opinion, expectations are part of the human condition. They are part of our striving to improve our capabilities. If human beings did not have expectations, we would not have evolved so far so rapidly. We are programmed to want to excel, to want to manifest, to want to be the best we can in whatever endeavour.

Of course, to a great extent it serves us to strive, but it is necessary to monitor the way in which we do this. There is nothing wrong, for example, with achieving something that seemed impossible, but if this occurs at the expense of others, it becomes unhealthy.

It is very easy to get caught in our own striving towards our own goals. Then if someone does not perform to how we think they 'should', we feel that it jeopardises our mission. But deep down we all know that life is not perfect and does not always go as we want it to. In order to manage these upsets and disappointments, we have to process them emotionally.

Expectations as emotional displacement

When we have an expectation of another person, unconsciously we are trying to change something about them as a way of displacing our own emotional discomfort. To counter this unhelpful behaviour, we need to become aware of what is triggering our feelings, and learn how to sit in our psychic and emotional discomfort. It is important to cultivate the ability to tolerate difference and accept people the way they are. It is not our task to try to change people and the world. All we can do is model healthy, respectful behaviour. When other people see us behaving in this way, they will change. It may sound incredible, but it's true.

EXERCISE
CHALLENGING YOUR EXPECTATIONS

Think of the expectations that you have of others. Now ask yourself the following questions of each expectation, writing the answers in your journal.

* Is this expectation reasonable?

* If yes, why?

•

Think of the expectations you have of yourself. For each expectation, ask yourself the above questions, again writing the answers in your journal.

•

Think of the expectations others have of you. Repeat the above process.

•

Think of the expectations others have of themselves. Repeat the above process.

— ⚡ —

The language of expectation

It is important to monitor our use of the word 'should'. When we place a 'should' in our communication of our experiences and thoughts, there is usually an expectation associated with it, often in the form of an assumed demand. 'Should' can imply that my way is better than your way, for example. Thus it limits our creativity or potential for resolving problems and conflict. 'Should' falls into the either/or way of thinking.

Consider how often you use the word 'should' in your conversations. Every time you do so, you impose a value judgement on yourself and others. Every value judgement you make can potentially trigger a reaction in someone else. If the underlying expectation concealed in your 'should' is deemed to be unreasonable by the other person, they may react defensively or angrily. In effect, your assumption is responsible for creating a potential conflict.

EXERCISE
EXPLORING YOUR 'SHOULDS'

Identify ten people you can ask for feedback about how they experience your expectations or 'shoulds'.

•

Find an appropriate moment to approach each of these people and ask for this feedback. Be open to what they say – you may discover things about yourself that you would not have otherwise have known. Don't see the feedback as a dig at you. It is important not to take it personally. This is one person's view of you, nothing more. They are simply giving you important information about how they see your behaviour, which will support you in becoming more emotionally literate.

•

After receiving each person's feedback, thank them for their frankness and honesty.

•

Take time to assimilate the feedback you have received, writing your discoveries and thoughts in your journal.

— ⚡ —

It can be helpful to rephrase 'should' sentences so that you can avoid imposing your demands and assumptions about what needs to happen. Useful alternatives are: 'could', 'it's possible', 'possibly', 'might', 'maybe', 'perhaps I could have'. For example:

'Should' sentence	**Alternative**
You should have been on time !	You could have tried to been on time.
You should behave yourself!	I feel scared when you behave like this.
You shouldn't speak to me like that.	Could you please speak to me respectfully?

In anger management the kind of language you use to express your reality, feelings, concerns and experiences is important in maintaining healthy relationships. When we are angry with someone and feel that they are disrespecting us, we need to be aware that by responding abusively we give our power to them. It is our task to remain as calm and adult as possible, rather than becoming regressed and retorting maliciously.

Letting go of our expectations can be profoundly transformative. As our 'shoulds' diminish, our need to be aggressive and hostile slowly dissolves too. Our task is to try to accept ourselves and others simply for who we are, moment to moment.

EXERCISE
LETTING GO OF YOUR
EXPECTATIONS

Make a list in your journal of the times when you have been
angry with others because of your expectations of them.

•

Now make a list of the times when you have become angry
because of the expectations you have had of yourself.

•

What do you think you have achieved by the high expectations that you have set for yourself and others?

•

Whenever you get into conflict with anyone, consider
whether you have expectations of yourself and of the other
party. Could there be another way?

— ⚡ —

It's almost humanly impossible not to have expectations. However,
if we consider the great saints and enlightened beings who have
lived on this planet, we will note that they all appear to have let go
of their expectations in some way at some stage in their lives.
Perhaps this is what enlightenment is all about – an almost
impossible achievement, but one that is still worth striving for,
especially if we want to control and express our anger appropriately.

Rule 8: Anger by appointment only

I recently learnt a skill that I like to call 'anger by appointment only'. It is very effective in personal and professional relationships where there is continuity and reciprocity and helps the exploder to contain and the imploder to assert themselves.

During my life as an exploder I believed that everything had to be said and dealt with in the moment. However, this often proved to be counter-productive for all parties concerned. Since then I have learned that timing is crucial. There is no point in trying to discuss an issue with someone when they are clearly not ready, unavailable, stressed out, or in a state of HALT (hungry, angry, lonely or tired). In this situation we need to set up a structure for communicating our distress and anger at a future time. This is where anger by appointment only comes in.

Under this rule, if you have an issue you need to discuss, you approach the person you need to discuss it with and politely make an appointment to do so at a mutually convenient time. It might sound something like this: 'I have an issue with you that I need to resolve. Do you have time to do it now? It will take about 15 minutes.' Then if it's not OK, you can negotiate a time that suits both both of you.)

When your appointment arrives, you can use the clearing process described on page 213. Once you have completed the process, you should make sure that there is no residual anger and give the other person time to respond and give you feedback. It's important that at this stage you do not react to what they are saying.

Anger by appointment helps us to focus on the issue at hand and deal with our anger in a mature and respectful way. When we speak in the heat of the moment, we are likely to be regressed, and what comes out of our mouths when we are in this state is often designed to hurt, maim, wound or kill. So wait until such time as you are in your adult and then communicate your feelings.

My Anger Contract
– Staying on Track

Managing your anger in the long term is going to take some
serious focus, concentration and intention on your part. It
will test your limits and take you to places inside yourself where you
have never been before. You are going to need all the help you can
get, and that includes all your own inner resources as well as outside
support.

In order to succeed in this task, you have to really want to change.
If you have read this far, you are probably desperate to manage your
anger and determined to change. This is a good starting point.
Desperation is motivational, and that is a good thing!

In order to help you stay on track, I have developed a personal
anger management contract that you make with yourself. In effect,
this is the rudder you'll use to steer your boat. By making this
contract, you are supporting your desire to actualise change in your
life. It's about taking yourself, your anger and your commitment to
managing it seriously.

If you were in an anger management group, you would have a
staunch bunch of fellow travellers holding you accountable and

supporting you on your personal hero's journey. I am hoping by this stage that you have your support network in place (and are using your journal and applying all the other key rules of anger management). If so, making this contract will affirm you in your commitment. If not, then making the contract will help to get you on track. Hopefully, it will also awaken your internal guardian, who will monitor your daily journey.

If you break your contract, don't punish yourself. Just re-commit to yourself and your support group. Don't give up. You may find that making this contract will be an effective catalyst for analysing your own resistance to change. Making change in your life, means taking responsibility for what you feel, what you think and how you behave. This is easy to read about, but actually doing it is much more difficult. While people in your life want you to change, they may be unaware that this means they will also have to change. It's important that they take this journey as seriously as you do and give you all the support you need. The changes you are making will enhance their quality of life as well as yours. If your loved ones are not supportive of your efforts to change, you will need to be clear that you have to undergo this process for your own wellbeing and decide whether you want to continue your relationship with them.

By staying on track – employing the eight golden rules of anger management, the clearing process, the detour method and all the other techniques described in this book – you make yourself more relaxed, confident and increase your self-esteem. People will feel safe around you and trust you. You will be healthier physically and emotionally and therefore more likely to bring abundance and prosperity into your life.

This anger management model outlined in this book changed my life. I am fortunate in that I teach the model on a daily basis and this keeps me in check. It will be a little more difficult for you to keep what you have learned in your awareness 24/7. You will need to remain vigilant, self-aware and conscious of all your feelings, thoughts, beliefs and behaviours. This will help to keep your shadow out in front of you so it can't continuously trip you up. All of this will require discipline at first, but after three months or so it will be assimilated into your daily life and will come to you more naturally.

When the going gets tough, remind yourself that you are not perfect and that you cannot do everything perfectly. That's OK. If you do find yourself reacting angrily, simply reflect on what you could have said or done differently, make your apologies, dust yourself off and start again. Remind yourself that eventually you will be the master of your anger rather than your anger being the master of you. It's only a matter of time – but you have to make the effort, no one else can do it for you.

Keep reminding yourself how good it feels to contain your anger successfully or assert yourself in a healthy way. Remember how happy that makes you feel. Well, that's what we want to achieve as permanently as possible.

Read and sign the following staying-on-track contract as soon as possible. Doing so will immediately increase your self-esteem because you are doing something for yourself and making a commitment. You should then find three people to witness the contract for you.

My Commitment to Managing My Anger

Name ....

1 As from today I am committed to expressing my anger in healthy and appropriate ways.

2 I commit to non-violence and will refrain from hurting others with my anger.

3 I commit to applying the eight golden rules of anger management.

4 I commit to calling my support buddies when I find that my
anger is getting out of control and exploring this with them
in detail.

5 I commit to taking responsibility for my feelings and actions
and to communicating my feelings whenever and wherever
possible.

6 I commit to reminding myself that in order to manage my
anger I need help and support from others.

7 I commit to writing in my journal on a regular basis, even if
it's just a few words on what has taken place during the day.

8 I commit to identifying what my main stress activators are
and reducing them from now on.

Signature: . . . .

Date: . . . .   Time: . . . .

Name of witness one: . . . .

Signature: . . . .

Name of witness two: . . . .

Signature: . . . .

Name of witness three: . . . .

Signature: . . . .

When you see the face of anger,
look behind it
and you will see the face of pride.
Bring anger and pride
under your feet, turn them into a ladder
and climb higher.
There is no peace until you become
their master.
Let go of anger; it may taste sweet
but it kills.
Don't become its victim.
You need humility to climb to freedom.

Jallaludin Rumi